Zesty Changes

~Get Up, Get Dressed, Get out~

by

Sharon North Pohl

www.ZestyChanges.com

ISBN: 9798386427818
Imprint: Independently published

Dedication

I dedicate this book to my birth daughter **Elliana Javed**. My biggest regret in life is not getting to know her until she was 23. My biggest joy in life is spending the rest of my life with this beautiful, courageous, zesty woman, who happens to be my daughter.

Table of Contents

Get Your Free Guide

Scan the QR code to get free tips, recipes, and guides.

Recognition

Co-Author, Producer, Big brother
There are lots of words and thoughts about how **Noel Murphy** has contributed to this book. I can't quite find the perfect one word. If he were a woman, I would call him a midwife because he helped me birth "Zesty Changes". He's been a Big Brother, inspirational coach, Co-author. He's been a producer. Noel is an award-winning filmmaker, and he approached this book like he would a film. I so appreciate his expertise, support, and even push when that's what it took. This book would not be here without Noel's dedication to Zest and his belief that the world is waiting for these healing stories.

Editing Team
As **Senior Editor**, self-professed high ranking member of the grammar police (she's at least a Captain), **Gunilla Leavitt,** wrangled commas, wrestled apostrophes, and otherwise made things read right and look pretty. Her attention to detail and her patience made an enormous difference.

Mary Nester was instrumental in structuring this book, and we would like to thank her for her brilliance. She brought the array of spices and assisted in creating the direction of the book.

National storytelling champion **Laura Packer** helped us identify the deeper strings of truth binding these stories and creating the flow.

The Story Contributors

Here is a huge shout-out to **all the brave, zesty women** who have shared their stories, triumphs, and struggles. You have inspired me to write this book. Each contributor dug deep into some painful memories, sometimes secret, never-told places, to reveal their stories. They all believe that it is powerful to shed light on dark times. Their collective belief is that you and the world will be better for sharing their triumphs over tragedy. Another woman, or man, may need to hear the story of their journey at just the right time, so we release the treasure chest to the Essence of Zest!

PROLOGUE

ZESTY CHANGES

~Get Up, Get Dressed, Get Out~

When we "**Get Up**", we take the first step in changing our circumstances. We physically get up out of those beds we believed we had to lie in. We toss aside the tired spiral of victimhood, anger, and revenge. We stretch, physically and mentally, to move energy forward. Getting up is always good. Its guiding principles are empowerment, positivity, and action, manifesting gently for your inner child. We want to go exploring. We want to see what comes next.

When we "**Get Dressed**", we celebrate our inner beauty. It is literally the practice of beautification, and it is not simply about the clothes we choose to wear. Getting dressed includes an awareness of our immediate surroundings, keeping a focus on the smallest detail, and finding a way to enhance the ambiance of everyday spaces. The result is the flow. We create rituals of rejuvenation for our minds, our bodies, and our spirits. When we get dressed, we commit to our own process of rebirth, health, and well-being.

When we "**Get Out**", we step into our chosen community. We reconnect with nature and are greeted with a fuller spectrum of possibilities. The blues are bluer, the greens are greener, and the future becomes brighter for it.

Our hippie generation, those of us who chose a better path and survived the allure of the drugs, made a huge difference in the world we live in today. We are now called the baby boomers and are pushing into our 70s and 80s. Many of us are still activists. Jane Fonda, for example, gained activist notoriety for her controversial anti-war position during the Vietnam war. She is now leading a very visible movement at the age of 83.

Jane is committed to raising awareness and is mobilizing a massive following to do something about climate change. Her civil disobedience is through demonstrations on the White House lawn that are called Fire Drill Fridays. Our earth is on fire. Her call to action once again has motivated me and thousands of my generation to get up, get out of our comfort zones, and get involved.

Today is the Day to move on. I encourage you to **Get Up, Get Dressed,** and **Get Out**. Whether things are dark or bright, we can always be and do a little bit more to enhance our Mojo. What are you passionate about? Where can you make a difference? Our world needs us to Get Up once again and engage full-out. A portion of the net proceeds from this book will go to organizations involved in environmental initiatives and programs to help unwed mothers.

-Sharon North Pohl

PART ONE: GET UP

"You don't learn from successes; you don't learn from awards; you don't learn from celebrity; you only learn from wounds and scars and mistakes and failures. And that's the truth."

—Jane Fonda

1. Susie Butterfly: The Chrysalis

Savory

"It's never too late - never too late to start over, never too late to be happy."

-Jane Fonda

I am 67 years of age, and I have just written, published, and marketed my first book, *Butterflies and Baked Beans*. It's never too late to write that book you have in you!

My story really started when I was 40, and my husband called me, crying, while I was doing the ironing. He said to me, "You know, you're much too bright to stay at home. Our kids are all in school, so you actually have no excuse to stay at home now. You need to go out there..." Then he said, "Go and finish the degree that you started 20 years ago."

I went and registered at a local college. My three daughters were ages 6, 10, and 12 at that point, and I enrolled for a science degree (of all things) because I wanted to understand the impact of science and technology on society. That's what the degree was about. My desire was to learn more about computers because I could see that they were going to change all our lives. I wanted to teach my daughters so that they would have the tools to empower themselves, just like I did.

I got my degree, a first-class honors degree. I was so excited by all the things that I discovered that every time I came home, I'd ask them, "What did you learn in school today?" They would tell me, and then I would say, "This is what I picked up at the university."

They were so inspired that my 12-year-old daughter went in for a national newspaper competition in London a year later. She won the prize to go to Moscow to Star City to see the launch of the Juno spacecraft with the first female astronaut, Helen Charmin. That was absolutely amazing and something neither of us would have even dared to imagine! The following year her younger sister, who was 10, decided she'd go in for the competition. She won first prize, which was to take her entire class for a dream day in London, and what a day we all had!

What I'm saying is that by going and doing the degree, I got the confidence to get back into the workplace. This was a very good thing because when I was 42, just after I graduated, I found my husband dead. He was 46. I went to find out if he had finished the cup of coffee that I'd taken him. He was going to look after the girls while I went for a big job interview with the university, and just like that my life was turned upside down.

If I hadn't gotten that degree, and if I didn't have the confidence, I don't know what I would have done or how I would have raised my girls. But I had the degree, and I did raise my children.

I think I managed because I am an optimist and because I live my life with zest. No matter what life throws at me, I find a way to get around it. Somehow, I find myself in a state of grace where I just keep going.

I think that if you educate a woman, particularly a mother, you are not just educating her and her children - you are educating their friends, along with the rest of the village, tribe, or community. Educate mature women! I got so much more out of school when I was getting my degree at 40 than I did when I tried, and then dropped out, at 20.

That's my story. My zest for living has taken a beating over the years, but it has never gone away.

"When a caterpillar "gets up" in the morning, it has no idea at all of what's to come. That little fella has to have enough movement to spark his destiny. Even nature shows us that we must awaken first and then get dressed. No human fashion designer ever topped the Ritz put on by a butterfly."

-Sharon North Pohl

2. Dee C:
Hearts and Stories

Peppermint

"The world needs your story in order to be complete."

- Anne Jackson

I have several different passions in life. The main thing I want to do is encourage people to operate in their purpose and know that they were put on this earth for a particular reason. Mine is to help people tell their stories.

I love to help people explore that by publishing the work of others into books. Everyone has their own message. It's their story, their voice, and it doesn't matter what type of book it is! It could be a children's book, a cookbook, a how-to book. It could be a personal memoir, an inspirational book, a collection of poetry. No matter what it may be, it is something uniquely placed inside of you, and the world is waiting for it. Other people may do the same thing you do, but nobody has your exact message.

That's what makes it so powerful. There is somebody out there that needs your message, so I work with people to bring it out.

Are you happy and fulfilled in your life with what you are doing? At any point in your life, you can reinvent yourself and decide that "this is the direction I want to go. This is the dream that I have that I'm following".

While you're doing that, even though that is a wonderful thing, and it is the first step, you want to make sure that you keep going even though there will be discouragement along the way. There are going to be obstacles. You are going to get knocked down and have days where you want to give up.

As you know, they say, "quitters never win and winners never quit." The most important thing is that no matter what you face on a daily basis, or what you experience in your life, when you fall, you get back up. Your pain is a key to what your purpose is.

Never quit. I say that with a smile on my face because I almost did a bunch of times! When I felt down and wanted to give up, I felt so many things for so long that I began to wonder, "Is this ever really going to change?" I would have people saying, "Well, you can't give up, you know, don't give up!" or whatever. And I would say, "Well, I understand that, but you don't know it from my perspective; you haven't failed as many times as I have." Sound familiar?

When you are alone, by yourself, in the dark with the blinds drawn and the curtains pulled, and it's just you, all you want to do is pull the covers over your head. You don't want to get up, don't want to talk to another person, you don't want to try another day. Maybe you don't know what to do, and you just wonder, "How can I even make it to the next hour, or to the next day?" I've been there, and I forged my way out.

I have mentors in my life, voices speaking into my ear. What goes into your ear is very important. I truly believe that faith comes by listening. What you pick up on can change absolutely everything.

I jumped on YouTube sometimes to find inspirational and motivational videos, and I would stick the earbuds in my ears and play the videos over and over. I listened to the same thing, and it just kept getting better and better. Then, before I knew it, I was opening the curtains, I was raising the blinds, I was getting dressed. And then, I was motivated to continue to go on.

The things that you go through are what help you live the brilliant masterpiece that is your life. Obstacles will come into your pathway; you will struggle, and because of what you have gone through, you will be able to use your experience to build and grow.

One of the things I would do is look at other people's inspirational stories for people who were failures and then became successful. For example, I found out that Steven Spielberg got rejected from film school three times only to become one of the greatest and most successful filmmakers of all time. Michael Jordan got cut from his high school basketball team, and that's completely ironic now, as he is now one of the best players ever to play the game!

One of my favorites is Babe Ruth. Most people know Babe Ruth as the "Homerun King," but many people don't realize that he's also the Strikeout King. I realized you've got to be willing to swing more than anybody else to knock it out of the park in life.

The things that you go through are what help you live the brilliant masterpiece that is your life. Obstacles will come into your pathway; you will struggle, and because of what you have gone through, you will be able to use your experience to build and grow. So, get back up. I know that it's hard, but just keep getting up! I guarantee that one day, you are going to get up, and you will find yourself in a position of success. It starts with telling your story.

"The story of the world is inside of you. Have you told it? If you hide your light under a bushel, you've lost something kind of crucial, dontcha think? "Get up!" is a battle cry for

what is possible. It's going from depletion and a heaviness to the UP. Up is a direction I follow in the faithfulness that I must saddle up before getting up on my horse. Some days? My horse just takes me somewhere new, and all I had to do was saddle up and get up. Wow, that easy? Yup. I mean Giddy up."

–Sharon North Pohl

3. Christine: What Was Once Down

"Always dare to dream. For as long as there's a dream, there is hope, and as long as there is hope, there is joy in living."

- Invajy

I'm a negotiation consultant. The cathartic part of my story took place when I was 19. I had this very successful high school career, beauty queen, top speaker, honor student, etc. In Montana, where I'm from, I got scholarships to college, and that's where things fell apart.

I went to the same college as my high school boyfriend. He joined a fraternity and decided to start moving in a different direction, so we broke up. I had been dealing with a bunch of issues, and to me, it is very interesting how our stories unfold.

At 16, a "friend" raped me, and I never dealt with it. It happened, and then just 10 minutes later, I had to meet with a high school teacher and other girls, and so I just shoved it down inside. Well, that ended up playing out after I broke up with my boyfriend. After that, I became incredibly promiscuous; I would sleep with anyone. By then, I believed that the only reason I was on the planet was to please men sexually, so that's what I did.

I wanted to become a newscaster. That's what my dream was—to be a television newscaster. Barbara Walters was my heroine. I loved her and Leslie Stahl, and that entrepreneurial, pioneering group of women in the media.

I ended up meeting this guy I wasn't interested in, but eventually, I did go out with him. A couple of months later, I was pregnant. All of the things I had dreamed of being came crashing down.

The day I found out that I was pregnant, I went home and broke every album I owned. I smashed my beauty queen tiara, destroyed all my speaking trophies. I broke everything because I didn't deserve any of it. I felt that I had become my mother's worst nightmare, which was me becoming an unwed teen mom. I was 19. Therefore, I was useless. I was nothing, and I was not qualified to make decisions for myself.

In the middle of all of this, I was running for political office. I ran for committee ward chairperson and won when I was 18. I was very involved in my political party and was helping run a campaign at the time.

I had all these things happening, found out that I was pregnant, and lost my job.

I quit school, got evicted from my house, and lived in a little tiny trailer in a trailer park. That's what I had become; I was the stereotypical trash at that point. Even then, I got evicted from my trailer.

I had no place to go, so in the dead of winter, as I crammed my belongings and my cat into my 1972 Chrysler Newport, a woman in my trailer park took pity on me and invited me to stay with her. This was a double blessing as she, too, was pregnant. What I didn't realize was that she was also a heroin addict.

One night, she had a group of people come to the house, and they were shooting up. I remember lying in the closet that was my bedroom with the pillow just over my ears so I couldn't hear. It was very upsetting. I still remember hearing her as she was shooting up, knowing that a baby would be born into that. She eventually got in trouble and kicked me out. She kept my stereo and some of my other belongings.

I was in the back in my car with my cat and surviving possessions. I was part of "The Hidden Homeless." I was walking one day; I had just gotten a job at McDonald's. I hadn't told them that I was pregnant, and I was terrified of doing so because I was afraid they were going to fire me—this was in the mid-80s.

I saw this frat guy that I had known. "What's new?" he asks, and I'm like, "Well, I'm pregnant." That was the start of our relationship. He needed to rescue somebody, and I needed to be rescued.

We got married. It started out okay, but then it started to morph into this very controlling situation where I couldn't be smarter than he was at something; I couldn't be better than he was at anything.

He started out being good with my daughter. At this point, I am 20, I have a baby, and I am pregnant with my second child. He can't get a job. I needed to get out of Montana, I didn't like it there. So I took an atlas, I opened it, I closed my eyes, took my finger, and just circled around the atlas and hit Boston. We decided to move to Boston. He was going to work for a Boy Scout camp for the summer, working on the waterfront teaching kids how to swim. My second daughter was born at the end of May, and after that, he left for Massachusetts.

A few weeks later, my daughters and I fly out with my mom, and I think he will be there to pick me up. He is simply not there. He is not to be found at all, which my mom saw and nearly put me back on a plane. Eventually, I went down to the waterfront to find him, and this tall, geeky guy with a mullet tells me my husband left town.

Later I found him. Then I finally wrote in my diary that I had married the wrong man. However, I did not believe in divorce, so that was that.

Fast forward, my husband could not get a job, so he took a position working full time for the Boy Scouts. We moved to upstate New York, and life went to hell because we couldn't afford to feed ourselves.

He did not believe that women should work. I looked like June Cleaver, but behind the scenes, he started to get violent. We got involved in a church that believed that I should be subservient to my husband and that if anything was wrong in the house, it was my fault. If only I tried harder, if I had more sex whenever he wanted, if I had the girls dressed nicely and dinner on the table, then it would be better, and all that was on me.

Then I got pregnant again.

Now I've got a third kid coming. He finally acquiesces and agrees to let me work, and I go back to working at McDonald's. It just kept getting worse and worse and worse until finally, we moved back to Massachusetts.

I'm 22 years old with a three-year-old, a two-year-old, and a one-year-old. I am going nuts, and I've got to go to school. I have got to get myself to school! I have always wanted to earn an education; it has always been profoundly important to me. He was somebody who would build me up and then pull the rug out from under me at the last minute, and then try to pick up the pieces.

I declared "I've got to go to school." I applied to college, and I got waitlisted. A couple of days before I registered, he lost his grip, broke every dish in the house, and then he hit me. I called one of my girlfriends, who is the most intense abuse survivor I have ever known, and she said to me, "Christine, how important is it that you go to school?" I said, "It's very important." She said, "Well, what's the worst thing he's going to do if you go anyway?" I was like, "Is he going to kill me? No."

"Then how important is school?"

I got a full-ride scholarship to a school called Rensselaer Polytechnic Institute. It was an engineering school.

While I was going to school, I wasn't allowed to study when he or the girls were awake. I'd get up at three or four in the morning and study. I'd go to school, come home, make sure everything was cooked and on the table. I did all that crap and still got a scholarship to go to Rensselaer.

I walked onto campus. I remember the day; it was August 28th. I looked around, and I said, "This is going to be easier without him than with him." I went home, threw all his shit on the front yard, and said, "I'm done."

I moved my daughters and myself to upstate New York and became the first woman to graduate as a single mom and full-time student at Rensselaer, where there were only 20% to 23% women to begin with. In the end, I got a 4.0.

I got a high-paying job. In my undergrad, I ended up working at what is now Verizon, doing international mergers and acquisitions, traveling all over the world.

I decided I wanted to go to business school. I only applied to one school, and that was it, because it was the only school that everybody knew, no matter where I was in the world. I applied to Harvard University. In one of my essays, which was describing a time when you lead a group of people through change, I wrote about leading my daughters through a divorce, and what it was like to be homeless and living in that situation. I got in.

I married the geeky guy with the mullet and the rat tail six years later, and we've been married for almost 30 years. I have been building this amazing career. What I have learned is how to negotiate with myself and negotiate with others, but from a place of not having power. In my profession, people talk a lot about leverage. Frequently I have gone, "What's that?" Because often, I have not had leverage. Figuring out how to find it and create it, and then believing enough that I have it to be able to exercise it to get what I want and what I need, has been huge. It has also given me a different type of empathy.

I don't care about people's histories. I just don't. I care only insofar as they have helped a person to grow and be human. I'm very passionate about leveling the playing field between people, and it took 10 years to make that happen. I have this philosophy that you cannot truly understand what it means to give until you have been forced to be in a position to receive. Without those ten years, I would never have learned that lesson, and that lesson drives everything I do in my life.

"Humility is not thinking less of myself; it's thinking of myself less. I am really wasting precious time and resources by not wearing my crown. My crown is not heavy, because it's the available love I have to give. All I need then is a receiver."

-Sharon North Pohl

What Was Once Down

4. Tracey F: Up Struggle

Oregano

"Develop success from failures. Discouragement and failure are two of the surest steppingstones to success."

- Dale Carnegie

When I was 18 years old, I was diagnosed with osteosarcoma, also known as bone cancer. It is a very painful, intrusive cancer that targets the young. Oh, before I forget, I was also six months pregnant, married, and had a 10-month-old.

My doctor advised me to terminate my pregnancy. I refused, which forced him to come up with another treatment plan. He told me that if I waited three more weeks, until I hit the 3rd trimester, to start chemo, my baby would likely survive, but he couldn't give me any guarantees as to what chemo might do to her.

I was scheduled to be admitted to MD Anderson Cancer Center on 9/11/01. Yes, the day our country stood still. The day our lives changed forever, and the day we will never forget. While the world was glued to their tv screens and my country was preparing to go to war, I too was under attack and preparing for the biggest battle of my life.

After my first round of chemo, my husband left me. I have no hard feelings towards him. He was young too. He did the best he could under horrible circumstances. I filed for a divorce.

With my daughter being six weeks early, she stayed in the NICU while I headed back to the purple floors of MDACC to do one more round before enduring a 13-hour limb salvage surgery.

We brought in 2002 with more chemo and all the side effects possible. I dealt with low blood pressure, kidney failure, mouth sores so painful I could barely eat or drink. I was overdosed on chemo to the point that I lost my motor skills for a day. I was on crutches for ten months. I became addicted to the pain meds they gave me. The list goes on.

The chemo was slowly killing me, and I knew if I finished those last few rounds, I would die. After over a year of being told I had cancer, I decided no more.

Going to war with cancer beat me up pretty good. But if I could go back and change it, I wouldn't. I took way too much from that experience. I went from being a girl who hated struggles to embracing them. Instead of allowing my struggles to take from me, now I take from them and use them in a way that serves me. I have learned that struggles are simply growth opportunities in disguise. They are meant to give us experience and help us grow.

I'm just a girl from Texas who realized that struggles are for me, not against me, if I choose. Struggles are universal. No one will ever go through life struggle free. So why not embrace them? Why not learn from them? Why not grow? Because in the end, struggles really can lead to happiness.

"Our struggles don't define us, but they mold us into stronger and wiser people. It's time to let go of the anger and resentment we feel around our struggles and take a look at how they've transformed us into better people."

-Sharon North Pohl

5. Merri-Jo: Forgiving the Unforgivable

Clove

"Darkness cannot drive out darkness; only light can do that. Hate cannot drive out hate; only love can do that." -Martin Luther King, Jr.

My brother's wife shot and killed him, and I forgave her.

I'm going to share with you a story of my life that had a major impact on me. When I was in my 40s, my brother was shot and killed by his wife. He was my favorite sibling and meant so much to me. I heard about it by way of a phone call when I was out speaking on a stage, about 300 miles away from home.

My first reaction was just how could this happen? I ended up in a church, screaming at God, just saying, "How do you let this happen? My brother was just like Jesus walking on earth. He was so precious, and he has two beautiful children, 14 and 16." I was so angry, and I just screamed. Because, you know, God tells us he wants to hear from us. He didn't specify how we had to behave, he just wants to hear from us.

He heard from me that night. I just went at it for about two and a half, three hours until I was so spent, I was just drained. After that, I went back to the women's house where I was staying and made arrangements to fly out the next day so I could take care of everything.

When I woke up in the morning, I had this incredible sense of total forgiveness come over me. The Lord placed a picture in my mind: these kids were going to be mine. I flew back out to Mammoth Lakes, California. I live in Dallas, so that was quite a distance. Joining the community out there, I went to the jail where my sister-in-law was held. I prayed with her and told her I loved her, and I gave her some money because she didn't have any.

Driving back to the kids I said to myself, “What the heck was that?” It's a behavior you don't believe can exist. But the strength the Lord had given me allowed me to forgive her, and walk forward, and do all the planning for the funeral and everything else that was going on.

After the funeral was over, there was an article in the paper that really touched my heart. The whole community of Mammoth Lakes wrote up that they were expecting the Lao family (my family, that's my maiden name) to come into town, and they were going to just hug on us and love on us, and allow us to know that they loved us and cared for us to dissipate our pain, when in fact, we came into town, and we nurtured them. That was so touching to me that we can have an impact on an entire community.

Of course, I did take the kids back to Dallas. I let them finish out their school year a month later and came back to town and packed up the house. We had a rummage sale, and I took them across the country in a van. I told them, "This is where I am with my feelings about your mom and what's happened." I said, "When you are ready to forgive your mom, I want to start flying out to California to visit her in prison."

It has been an incredible journey. The kids graduated from high school. I sent them off to college, and they graduated from that. Both are married, one has two children. You can hardly believe the trauma that these two children have avoided! They are doing incredibly well.

Their mother just got out of prison two years ago. She is now living in a place that we found for her here in the Dallas area. I live about 50 miles away from her, and she got a job that we helped her get. We are trying to have her settle back into society after 18 years in jail.

Know that whatever circumstances you are under, you are at choice. Don't worry about what society tells you to behave like or what the laws say; you're at choice about how you respond to things that happen to you. You can choose to come from what I call 'responsible' or 'able to respond,' or you can choose to be a victim.

I always look back at these kids, and I think, what if I had chosen to hate their mom for the next 20 years? How would these children have turned out? There are always consequences to the choices we make. I just encourage you to make a great choice.

"I think I was born old and get younger all the time. I think that the universe loves me and wants me to succeed. What I choose to be, I become through my self-care and allowing others to support me."

-Sharon North Pohl

6. Sandy: This Is Not My Movie

Borage

"Expectations were like fine pottery. The harder you held them, the more likely they were to crack."

-Brandon Sanderson, The Way of Kings

This was not how it was supposed to be! As I listened to the surgeon, my brain could not process what he was saying. Inoperable? Rare? Peritoneal? What did it all mean?

Basically, what it meant was that I was going to lose my husband, my partner, my best friend. He was only 55 years old, he was never sick, and now he was dying? We were going to spend our old age together! Now we were never going to get there. Gene was diagnosed with peritoneal cancer, a rare and terminal cancer with a survival prognosis of about three months.

However, he was a fighter, and we explored many different options before deciding on a course of treatment. It was a battle we would face together, and we were lucky to have an oncologist who genuinely cared about us.

Gene lived for 14 months after his diagnosis. None of them were easy months, and some were much more difficult than we ever expected, but until the last three months, he was able to enjoy his life despite his illness. He lived to see his fourth and final grandchild born. He was able to attend the weddings of his niece and his nephew and was able to continue to work for a while and interact with family and friends.

Our life became about doctor visits, chemo treatments, hospital stays, and prescription drugs. Without a doubt, it was the most challenging year of our lives. But God was good to us. He blessed us with an incredible support group of family and friends, and He brought us new friends through the experience.

Gene was one of the most incredible, strong, brave, positive people I have ever known. Someone close to him commented, "Gene sets the standard for how to behave with a life-threatening illness." One of his doctors said, "Gene is an impeccable, incredible example of what a human being should be."

What a lucky woman I was to be loved by such a man! How could I ever survive such a loss? Deep in my heart, I knew that I was going to lose him. I believe I knew that from day one, even though I thought that if anyone could beat this disease, it would be Gene.

But that was not to be. On May 18, 2004, God called Gene home. His last few days were such a struggle for him that it was a blessing for his agony to end. He was ready to go home…he told me that the day before he died. He died peacefully at home, surrounded by his family, and that was his final blessing on this earth.

My heart was broken. Shattered. There are no words to describe how I felt. We had the most incredible love for each other, and we were so blessed in so many ways. I was lost, adrift, not sure what to do with myself. Most days, I didn't even want to get out of bed. But several things kept me going.

Gene asked very few things from me before he died, but one of them was a promise that I would be okay. I made that promise to him, and I meant it. I forced myself to do the same normal things that people do, because I promised I would be okay. I got dressed, I cleaned my house, I went grocery shopping, I played with my grandchildren. I paid my bills, decorated for the holidays, went to lunch with friends.

Each day got a little easier, and finally, there was a time when I really was okay – even if it was only for an hour out of the day. I was getting there.

Secondly, shortly after he was diagnosed, Gene realized what a financial burden a cancer diagnosis could be on families with limited incomes. In keeping with the kind of man he was, he decided there had to be a way to provide help directly to these people. He told me that he was going to throw a big birthday party for himself and ask everyone to bring donations to help other people.

That idea was the basis for Gene's final legacy – The Gene Roman Family Foundation. As of this writing, we are planning our 18th Annual Fundraiser and have helped over 500 individual cancer patients struggling to pay their daily living expenses during treatment. I am proud to be the Executive Director of this foundation, with a wonderful board of directors made up of other family members.

Third, I had four little grandchildren, ranging in age from 10 months to four years old. I was blessed that they lived close to me, and I was able to spend lots of time with them. The innocence, unconditional love, and unwavering trust of little children never fail to warm the heart. Those four little guys probably had tons of hugs and kisses, and they really helped me feel better.

When you love someone, and they die, you never 'get over it.' It's never really 'okay.' But I found I could indeed go on, grateful for the time we had together, for our love for each other, and for our faith in God's plan.

Did I understand that plan? Did I like it? No. But I trusted God and his plan for the rest of my life.

"Grief is like autumn; it is a season changing. Welcome it, find out what it wants from you, sit with it, then bid it a safe ride and lock the door after it leaves."

-Sharon North Pohl

7. Tracy B: Tragedy to Triumph

"A mother is always patient. A mother is always kind. A mother is always giving. A mother never falls apart. A mother is the buffer between her child and the cruel world."

-Jessamine Chan, The School for Good Mothers

I am an author and a mom, and I live in Denver, Colorado. I am the founder of a nonprofit known as The Lightest Path to Healing Foundation. I want to start my story by giving you a little bit of background on me.

Back in 1992, I was going through a divorce, and I decided to go into the fitness industry because it was a passion and a love of mine. Despite being in my dream job, I was going through a tough time. One day in the middle of a training session with a woman, I just heard something in my spirit say, "Take care of that. I made that."

It changed my vision of the people who walked in the door. I saw them as this amazing miracle, a true gift. I saw them for who they really were and how defeated they were.

Fast forward to when I was 36 years old. I had been married to a man, my best friend, and he started becoming a little different. We were business partners; we owned three large fitness facilities here in Denver. We had 15,000 members; it was a big business. We did this thing together, just as we did life together. We had a miracle baby, Elijah, after I was cured of endometriosis. This was back when he was 8 or 9.

My husband started to change and do some funny things. We couldn't figure it out. We went to doctors, but to make a long story short, when you witness your best friend and husband change right before your eyes, having no idea what is going on is very traumatic. For myself and my son, I know for a fact that it was.

We had gone through this for about five years, back and forth, trying to figure out what was wrong with him, when we found out he had a brain disease. He had become very abusive, yet he had control over our business. Then he was phased out, became hostile, and turned into something that I didn't understand. He had never shown a side like that before. There was a part of his brain that literally ate the part controlling reason. It was like he was just this shell of a man, and he had absolutely no idea.

Two weeks before he died, we found out it was Jacob's disease, which is a form of cow disease. He was a champion athlete, and he took a drug in 1977, a performance-enhancing drug, never suspecting that it would kill him decades later.

They now call it the decades disease. It is a very slow-moving disease that eats up the brain on the inside and gets fast-moving right before the end. I was grateful for the diagnosis, as it made me understand what was going on. I don't know about you, but understanding something really helps me in the healing process, so that was a gift in itself.

The night before he died, we went to the hospice. My little boy was sitting in the corner of the room. The reason I'm telling you this is because it's been a huge part of me coming through this story. This was a 12-year process that I've gone through, and it's so much better on the other side.

The night that he died, I went in, and I finally said goodbye. While I was there, I fell asleep and fell into a very deep sleep. When you're going through something like that, you typically don't sleep so well. Well, this was a moment where I did. A couple of my family members were sitting at the bottom of the bed.

The room was dark, and my son was sitting in the corner. This big bright light came right over him. There was a section that was next to him. We didn't know what was happening at that point, but my mom took a picture, and we went home.

The following morning I got the phone call that my husband had died. I drove back to the hospice. Once I got there, I had this aha moment of "Oh, my gosh, I have to tell my son that his daddy's dead." It was two days before Christmas, so the timing couldn't be worse. I'm a person of faith, and while driving home, I was praying and going," Lord, how do I do this?"

I walked up the stairs to my son's room, put this limp, sleeping body on my lap, and I looked him in the face. I said, "Elijah, I have to tell you something about your dad." He looked at me and said, "What, mom?" I said, "Daddy died this morning about seven o'clock." He asked, "What time, mom?" I said, "About seven o'clock this morning." He said, "No, mom, daddy died about three o'clock last night when we were at the hospice. He looked good. He was surrounded by angels, and he told me everything was going to be okay. Can I have a donut?" and he ran off.

I found myself being a single mother and owner of a very large business, trying to juggle all this and help put together all the pieces. There was a time about nine months after my husband died, where I was just really at a low point.

Around October, I just felt something in my heart say, "Get up." I had to get up, and I had to decide at that moment, here is the fork in the road for me. At that moment, I was 43 years old, and I'm 50 now. I had to decide, "What do you want, Tracy? What do you want for you and your son?" I had to begin with the end in mind.

Something sparked inside of me because, during this journey, I found how alone my son and I were and how misunderstood we both were in this whole thing. We have started a foundation called the Lightest Path to Healing Foundation, and the theme is that you are not alone. We make sure that people know that they are not alone when they lose a loved one, like we have.

We are bringing experts and all kinds of people together, as well as the community, to let these people know that there is somebody, somewhere, who completely understands the journey they're on, and also to teach the community how to wrap their arms around these folks that are going through so much. Because, I have to tell you, I felt so invisible. Both my son and I do not want that to happen. We have even found that for kids, grief is so misunderstood. My son was bullied terribly at school.

With the facts in place, we know now that nobody in the school system knows what to do with children in grief; they really do not understand this thing. They avoid the elephant in the room and don't say anything. Kids are afraid that just by associating with other kids that this has happened to, they're going to catch it like a cold.

Elijah and I are on a quest, turning our tragedy into triumph. We are going to take this thing by storm and go set up communities all over the country, eventually the world, and make this place a better place, so these young men and women know that they are not alone, that they do have a future, and that they can finish well.

"Our hardest experiences are often the things we think we can't come back from. That's true. We can't be the person we were before. But we can move forward and use what we've learned to create fruitful, zesty lives. We can be better for ourselves and the ones we love most."

-Sharon North Pohl

8. Melinda: How am I needed?

Cinnamon

"Do you not see how necessary a world of pains and troubles is to school an intelligence and make it a soul?"

-John Keats, Letters of John Keats

One of my favorite coaches in basketball brought her team from obscurity to fame with this one idea. I believe it was Chris Gobrecht. She was the Women's Basketball Coach at the University of Washington, and she was our keynote speaker at Cornish Graduation in the early 1990s.

The lackluster ladies had endured one embarrassment after another until Chris came along. She got to the root of what they had been thinking on the court:

"How do I look?"

Once they were willing to commit to instead playing from the question, "How am I needed?" they completely transformed their game!

I have found myself spinning over where this COVID-19 virus is taking us. It is ironic because I was openly declaring greater mastery over my clinical depression this winter. I was feeling both hopeful and confident, but with the sudden appearance of COVID-19 I have felt, at times, helpless, terrified, and super angry.

Just this morning, I lamented that I knew what my life purpose was a week ago, and I loved my journey - before this virus plague showed up. With all my fantasies of darkness and despair, I concluded that my new life purpose must be to trudge through the oncoming devastation as I did during 2008 through 2011. Like so many artists, I barely survived.

But "How am I needed???"!

I searched more deeply, then I reflected. Over the course of several decades, I have discovered a million different ways that creative expression can be a miraculous lifeline for myself and others. The GIFT of clinical depression has given me endless opportunities to learn how to find a bit of light in every darkness - and grab hold!!!! I have collected a lifetime of insights.

So, "How Am I Needed?"

Is anyone out there longing to do more of their own art? Are you looking to share experience, hope, and strength that might offer some relief from fear? Who isn't? Maybe we can help each other. Stay tuned!

"I want all of my sisters everywhere to know that I don't think we were ever separate to begin with, so we are essential to each other's emotional and spiritual survival."

-Sharon North Pohl

9. Noel: King Lessons. Now and Then.

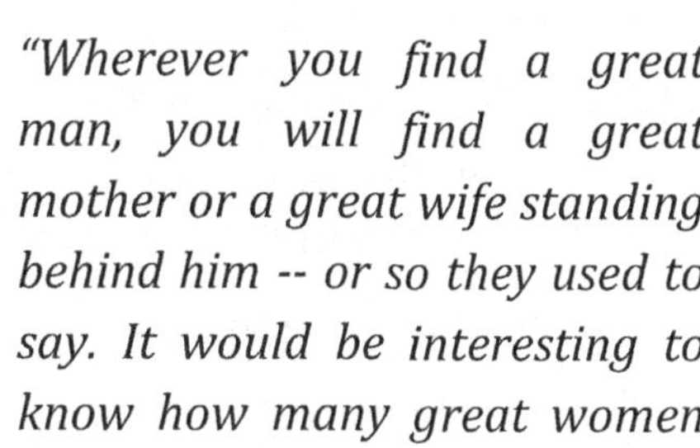

Arrowroot

"Wherever you find a great man, you will find a great mother or a great wife standing behind him -- or so they used to say. It would be interesting to know how many great women have had great fathers and husbands behind them."

-Dorothy L. Sayers, Gaudy Night

Let me explain how I became the only man to add to this book. I have had the privilege of "producing" this book from its inception. Yes, as a man! I have worked with many men and have been part of what some have called "The Men's Movement". I wrote a book of my own.

I met Sharon North Pohl in Santa Cruz, California, while media-coaching other coaches for TV and center stage appearances, pitching "what's possible". Sharon had owned a horse ranch and had been working with severely traumatized young women. The horse was the bridge, and Sharon was the conduit. She changed many young girls' lives and gave up a lot to do it. Later it cost her the ranch itself.

My favorite memory of Sharon is her and I speeding in her ranch truck, pulling an empty horse trailer straight into the wildfires in the Santa Cruz mountains to rescue gravely endangered horses. She is so fearless. She brings empathy to other women from the understanding of the strength it takes to get up off the mat and reconnect with that core determination.

She reminded me of the character Virginia Barkley from the TV show "The Big Valley", which I watched as a very little kid. I immediately saw the gentle and funny fierceness and just was kid-smitten out the gate. Sharon had a smart, protective energy.

Little did I know that I would become her mentor, and at times over the many years, she would occasionally find me stuck in that child state called "trauma". Sharon is acutely intuitive, and she would always find a way into what was going on with me. At times she's been my little sister, and other times my big sister, and I've been both her big and little brother.

One of her secrets with extended family like me is to share what's going on. For herself, she always clears the crap out and digs out her shine right in front of you. Unless? Yes, unless she is focused on you, in which case you are the only person in the world for her, and I am really starting to sound like an actual brother.

She quaintly calls this “zest”. It is more than zest. Zest is the result of the process of dumping old, negative stories and healing through self-kindness, self-care, and giving to others in your most unique way. It's uncovering the light under the bushel, and letting it shine. Sure, allure brings them in, but it’s zest that keeps them from drifting.

Zest is also “radiance”, which to me is when a woman owns her “inner Queen”. That’s the vibe we men love so much! It’s the secret vibe that has us wanting to build stuff for you, wanting to get the door for you, and more. We will open the door for you, but it’s your zest that has us looking forward to the next time we have the opportunity to hold the door for you. It's where allure brings you. We open up too, but zest is an inside job. All men can either see you owning your crown, with that radiance I mentioned, or not.

Many of my brothers have trouble accessing respectful behavior toward women unless it is CLEARLY asked of them. Women have been institutionalized to be afraid to ask men to have boundaries. This has no integrity and simply does not work.

As a very young child, I was in an orphanage. The concerned adults in my life at the time seemed to have other concerns, and I trusted neither men nor women. I had already been intimately abused by both by the time I was 6. I trusted Virginia Barkley though, I thought she was kick ass. And she looked so regal on that horse.

Do not think that was a crush, because my first crush was the Flying Nun. My young psyche must have decided that if a horse liked you, maybe you were safe? Either way, Westerns included this great woman, and one day I'd ride next to her, or maybe her daughter Audra.

My own mother was in the psychiatric hospital, and my father had his demons to contend with, so in 1965 I sat in my small, wooden chair in a room full of children who really didn't have parents and watched Virginia Barkley and her horse solve crimes. I was barely 6, and I was thrown before I could grow tall enough to make a respectable thud.

I understand hurt and resignation. I found that women told the truth to me if I was available to hear it. I thought men had no idea what feelings were. It was not the men, but the women, who stepped up and protected me. My story is interwoven in the fabric of what women have given to the world.

Women, as I would later find, would be the allies that saved me. It was women who took me from the ground to standing. It was these women who got me to get up. My god, nobody has thanked all these women for all the shit they have taken. So let me thank you because your sacrifices are in my fiber as a man. I can feel it, and I think that's why Sharon wanted me here.

My family of four older brothers and father were later reunited in Brookfield, Wisconsin, in 1967. I had severe headaches and stomach reflux, I had nightmares, and I sleep-walked as far as a mile from my home. I would wake up and not know where I was. I was so terrified all the time that that is what I would describe as normal. I had constant behavior problems and acted out pretty much all the time, so I was sent to special classes and schools.

When I was 10, I met a man who was not only a professor at the Harvard school of Divinity, but also a world-famous storyteller: Dr. Hugh Morgan Hill, Aka "Brother Blue". HE thought my behavior was just fine and took me with him to perform around Boston.

He put me on stage in front of faculty at Harvard and had me shake genuine slave chains at them, yelling and screaming for them to wake up to DISCRIMINATION. Wake up to idolatry of the shape and color, wake up to the suffering of women all over the world. Truly. I was 10, and I was chosen to ask them all to get up. See, this "Get Up" thing is a real thing... I know how to get up, especially when I'm sitting on railroad tracks and a train is coming.

Ruth Hill was the true fuel behind Brother Blue. She was my spiritual mother and Brother Blue was like a spiritual father. My skin was white; theirs was black. I had watched Dr. King's funeral on TV and could not understand why anyone would want to hurt them. Maybe because their skin is so beautiful? Ok, I was 10. I knew one thing, though: Get up, stand up.

One of my proudest moments later in life was presenting Ruth Hill onstage for her report on the Smithsonian's National African American Women's Oral History Project. As a man, to get this honor was enormous, and I got a free Museum coffee mug.

Finally, I want to mention that "getting up" counts as aerobic exercise; doubly so if you roar when you do it. I mean ROAR. Try it. Really. Start your day by roaring into it. After all, you are royalty, and the horns must sound when ZEST awakens!

I bow.

Noel Murphy

Thanks

-Sharon North Pohl

10. Sharon: Flashback! The story of my unbridled youth.

Lemon Zest

"There are no secrets that time does not reveal."

-Jean Racine

I was young in the sixties, when an entire generation was inspired to: ***"Get Up".*** I started high school in 1963. I was only 13 at the time and did not turn 14 for a few more months. One of my most powerful memories entering high school, was that of being so excited about all that was going on in the world, especially our youngest ever elected president, John F. Kennedy, 43 years old.

On November 22, 1963, I was hurrying to beat the bell into my freshman science class when a trembling voice came over the loudspeaker announcing that President Kennedy had been shot. The entire student body was grief-stricken. When I got to class, we were all hugging and crying together.

This fateful day ushered in the beginning of the anti-establishment movement of the tumultuous '60s. I was right smack dab in the middle of all of it. Racial tension was at an unprecedented high. Marquette Frye, a black man, was pulled over and arrested by a white Highway Patrol officer on suspicion of driving intoxicated. A crowd gathered, the situation escalated and triggered what is known as the Watts race riot. It went on for six days. Hundreds of buildings were burned. Entire city blocks were left in rubble and ashes by the angry mobs, kindled by years of racial inequality. 34 people died, over a thousand were injured, and $40 million worth of property was destroyed. This was only a year after the civil rights anti-segregation act of 1964 was passed. The saying of the times: *"Burn Baby Burn"*.

Half of the students in my high school in Sacramento were African American. My friends and my gym mates were of African descent. We staged demonstrations in solidarity with the riots in LA. Looking back on it, I didn't realize how segregated the Southern states were at that time. It didn't affect me in my school much, but it certainly affected my community. The race riots were a reflection of that civil unrest.

1964 was also the British invasion, the year that The Beatles first appeared on the Ed Sullivan Show, starting the whole flood of the British rock stars. Their music, long hair, and eccentric fashions electrified mobs of dedicated fans among the youth of America. The Rolling Stones, The Animals, The Kinks, The Who, The Dave Clark Five; Rock ruled the 6o's. They all came stomping, gyrating, and shaking into our lives at that time, helping to create the mentality of us vs. them. The electric music, dress, and long hair was a stark departure from the crooning artists and music of the '50s. Our dedication to following these rockers and their unconventional style helped distance our generation from our parents and the establishment. We were creating a new world. *"Don't trust anybody over 30."*

These times also saw the escalation of the Vietnam war. President Johnson increased the draft in 1965 from 17,000 a month to 40,000. In 1967, there were 500,000 troops in Vietnam. These young men, my friends turning 18, were being drafted every month. Many of my high school mates were being sent to fight the Viet-Kong. They ended up deep in the swamps and rivers of a small Asian country that they knew nothing about.

Coming back, there were no ticker-tape parades like the soldiers returning from WWII received. The Vietnam vets were met by a community that didn't believe in the war they fought so hard in. They were shunned. Many returning young soldiers came home with PTSD and addictions to stronger narcotics readily available in Vietnam, namely opium, hashish, and heroin. A lot of them became mentally compromised addicts, homeless casualties of the era.

It was a crazy time, and the Vietnam war was vastly unpopular with the youth. This spawned massive demonstrations, sit-ins, and civil disobedience. We rose up to object to the war in unprecedented numbers. I participated in many anti-war protests in this time of unbelievable social upheaval.

I started college at Sacramento City College in the fall of 1966. I was a 16-year-old high school graduate, turning 17 later in the year. At this point, girls were not allowed to wear pants to school, and skirts had to be to the knees. I helped organize a massive strike and sit-in at my college. Late in the fall semester of 1966, hundreds of us all wore our hip-hugging, bell-bottom jeans or short miniskirts to class. The anti-pants and long skirts rule was abandoned the following semester. It was unenforceable if the administration wanted to keep the school open and classes filled.

When I entered my psychology class in early 1967, I met a clean-cut, preppy young man named Gary. He had been his high school mascot, an Indian called Wampum Willie, hooting and hollering at the football games along with the cheerleaders. He was a handsome, popular figure.

We connected and debated about the things we were learning in our psych class. He was a gentleman; he carried my books for me. We started attending rallies together, and our friendship morphed into a girlfriend-boyfriend relationship.

The counterculture movement was gathering steam, and we were all in. He threw away his preppy clothes, grew his hair, started wearing a headband and bell-bottoms. We took trips together to rallies, concerts, and Haight-Ashbury, the legendary hippie mecca in San Francisco, California. We wore eccentric clothing with an ethnic flare: fabrics from India and Pakistan, embroidered blouses, no bra, bell-bottoms, lots of beads, flowers in our hair, and massive amounts of tribal-influenced jewelry. Peace symbols were on everything. We were the young counterculture visionaries, embracing world peace and love, and they called us hippies. Our parents were not happy with our new personas.

We covered our walls and ceilings with cotton tapestries and posters of our favorite rock bands. Complex Tibetan mandalas adorned with bright neon colors, and enhanced with blacklights, competed for space with flyers and mementos from marches, sit-ins, and demonstrations. Rock music was constantly blasting from vinyl records or 8 track tapes.

The first Whole Foods Store opened in downtown Sacramento, in a small, abandoned corner grocery store. I remember the creaky wooden floors and barrels of whole organic grains. We became vegetarians and juiced carrots until we turned orange from all the beta-carotene. We lived on greens and learned all about eating couscous, hummus, bulgur, mung beans, and every kind of soya product.

The great dichotomy of the era was the exploration of all kinds of drugs, while eating healthy, organic foods. Gary became more and more immersed in the drugs. There is a saying that goes, "At first, the man takes the drugs. Then, the drugs take the drugs. Finally, the drugs take the man."

That was certainly true for Gary. He began to create special blends of pot from different regions in Mexico. He became a connoisseur of different strains of Marijuana. His newfound expertise made him in demand, and he became a popular dealer of exotic weed. It wasn't long before he started experimenting with hallucinogens: peyote, psilocybin mushrooms, and LSD. Next came his use of amphetamines (uppers), and barbiturates (downers)

His personality was changing rapidly. He became extremely paranoid, started collecting and building weapons, primarily swords and knives of all types. He became fascinated with machetes, carrying one with him under the front seat of his hippie van, which was a big, red, retired ambulance.

I was done. The changes in his personality scared me. I broke up with him and proceeded to distance myself as much as possible. What I didn't know at the time was that Gary was extremely affected by his parents divorcing when he was young. He never told anyone his story, and he had never healed from the separation anxiety and feelings of abandonment.

When I split up with him, he had a complete mental breakdown. This was, no doubt, exacerbated by his use of methamphetamines and barbiturates. He was freaking out, having a bad trip. His mom called the police. They found him incoherent in his room, sitting in a pile of small pieces of my graduation photo. He had written "Love, Hate, why" over and over again, and ripped it up. They took him to the county psych ward. His sister had stashed his drugs, weapons, and money, or that bad trip would have been to jail instead of the hospital.

After that incident, he became increasingly obsessed with me. He was stalking me at school, calling all the time, showing up at my friends' houses. He followed me out of town and surprised me while I was staying with friends. He tried to get me to talk to him so he could lure me back. I avoided him, getting more and more scared. One time I was in his sister's car. He saw us, jumped in, and put a knife to my throat. His abandonment wound and the drugs had made him crazy. He believed he would only be sane again if he had me in his world.

This behavior continued into the spring of 1968. One day he came to my parents' home in the middle of the day while they were both at work. He was high on LSD and crying. He said he just needed to talk, and that he wouldn't hurt me. He pushed through the door, held a knife to me, and raped me, all the while crying and repeating over and over that, "now we are together again". I never told anyone at the time. I found myself pregnant from that one rape.

Abortion was illegal. My only choices were to either go to Mexico and risk death or go on a very expensive trip to Japan where abortion was legal. Neither was a viable option. I was left with telling my parents, and my enraged father kicked me out of the house.

The next day I left for Hawaii and spent two months on the north shore of Oahu with surfer friends. I landed with $50 in my pocket and a baby in my belly. I was depressed, estranged from my family, and feeling stuck in deep dark days of my soul. I had no idea what to do or where to turn next.

My sister, the epitome of the power of big sister energy, has always been there for me. She stayed in touch with me while I was in Hawaii and talked me into coming to Oregon to stay with her and have my baby. I flew back when I was almost six months pregnant.

-Sharon North Pohl

PART TWO: GET DRESSED

"Think like a queen. A queen is not afraid to fail. Failure is another steppingstone to greatness."

—Oprah Winfrey

Get Your Free Guide

Scan the QR code to get free tips, recipes, and guides.

www.zestychangecom/guide

11. Angel: Knife at My Throat

Turmeric

"The only person you have to blame is yourself when you could have made a different choice but instead you went against your gut feeling."

-Germany Kent

It was 2017. I was 45 years old and had hit that phase of my life where I was starting to gain some extra weight. I had that little belly forming, I was not sleeping well, and my metabolism seemed to be shutting down. I was recommended to see a hormone specialist, maybe lose 5 to 10 pounds, gain more mental clarity, etc.

I saw a highly recommended local doctor here in Denver, and we were just having the conversation about the stage of life that I was in. We were sitting at about eye level, and she asked me to look up. She had noticed a lump on my throat and asked me how long it had been like that. I really didn't know.

She immediately ordered tests. It was a Friday,

and she sent me for x-rays that afternoon. Before dinner, I got a phone call telling me she wanted a biopsy. There I was, standing in my kitchen, with a doctor calling after hours on a Friday, having said it would be a few days. My knees gave way. I was freaking out and imagining the worst.

I had multiple tumors on my thyroid. The biggest was five inches in diameter, pretty large for a butterfly-shaped gland inside your throat. By now, I saw it as clear as day, like there was a baseball in my throat every time I looked in the mirror. I never noticed it before, but there it was!

They sent me to a surgeon. Because of the size, they wanted to remove at least half my thyroid, if not the whole thing. At the time, I was a radio talk show host, hosting two back-to-back two-hour shows. Surgery would mean an extended absence from my radio show, as it would be impossible to go through all that treatment and still be on the air.

I decided to seek out multiple opinions. One of the best pieces of advice I got was from my chiropractor, who said, "You know, Angel, you probably have tumors because of inflammation. There are things that can be done to reduce inflammation, so let's try that first and see."

I had my doctors agree to give me a 90-day

window to see if we could reduce the inflammation in my body by changing my diet, adding vitamins, upping my nutrition, and really going into a lot of self-care. I started meditating and taking supplements. I stopped drinking white chocolate mochas from Starbucks every day and cut out sugar, caffeine, dairy, wheat, and alcohol, cold turkey. Boom!

My friends saw the dramatic shift in my choices and wondered how I had the willpower to give it all up. I remember saying to a girlfriend one time, *"It's easy when you have a knife at your throat."* That big scare is what it took for me to turn my life around, to recognize that we have control over our body, control over our aging. Our body is a temple, and it puts back out what we put into it.

Six months later, I had some blood work done. It all came back normal. The large tumor was still there, but the others had gone away. I was able to save my thyroid from surgery and improve my lifestyle and aging process, all at the same time.

I hope I never have a scare like that again, but that is what it took for me to make that change. It doesn't have to be that dramatic, but I think often we ignore the little signs and symptoms, thinking it won't make a difference. I am here to tell you: when you want it bad enough, it truly does make a difference.

"Listen to what your body is telling you. It may even say, "I love you and thank you for the self-care." Yup, your body could also just be thanking you by giving you a great day..."

-Sharon North Pohl

12. Susan: The Day You Are Truly Free

"You're not a victim for sharing your story. You are a survivor setting the world on fire with your truth. And you never know who needs your light, your warmth and raging courage."
-Alex Elle

Hi, I am Susan Bennie from Edmonton, Alberta, Canada, and you are not your story.

When I say that, I mean you are really not the story you tell yourself. So often, as women, we tell ourselves a story about why we can't do something.

For me, it started 24 years ago, when my daughter was born. She was born with a disability. The doctors told me that she can't walk, she can't crawl, she can't run, she can't eat by herself, she can't dress herself. I said, "No, not yet. But I will teach her, and she can." I took the word can't out of her vocabulary.

While I was doing that, I worked in a job where I was told every day that there were things I couldn't do. “Susan, you can't speak from your heart. You can't write a letter to save your life. You can't do things the way you want. You can't use your own brain. You can't use your own voice.” I got stuck in that, not realizing I was stuck because, for me, it was all about her and not about me.

Years later, I was laid off from my job when they downsized. 17 years had passed, and my daughter knew at that time that she could do anything she wanted. If she walked up here behind me, nobody would even know that she had a disability. She has risen above and can do anything she wants to do in this world.

But I was stuck. I looked at my situation and thought, “if I could take the word can't out of her vocabulary, certainly I can take it out of my own”. I had to relearn that. I had to figure out what I wanted to do and how I wanted to do it.

Working for somebody else, being told what you can and cannot do, is difficult. The day you realize that you must step out and be who you can be, do what you choose to do, and enjoy life, that's the day you're truly free.

There are days, good days, bad days. On a bad day, one when I say I can't do something, I catch myself and realize that I can do it. But it is my daughter who says to me every day, "Mom, yes, you can. Yes, you will, because yes, you are." She got that from me, because that's what I coach my people to do.

It's the story that we tell ourselves about how we get stuck, and it's about "Yes, I can, so can you." It's about "Yes, I can."

Yes, you can, what? Write it down, declare it, make it happen. You will do WHAT to make that happen? Because yes, you are. What are you? Say it as if it already exists! And repeat after me every day and tell yourself, "Yes, I can."

Then the stories you tell others about who you are and what you do become very, very powerful.

But know that the story you tell yourself every day is what will continue carrying on that zest for the future into a life of happiness, a life that you want, a life that you choose because you can do anything you set your mind to. You will do anything that you are able to do once you set your mind to it. You are a woman of power, you are successful, and you can do anything in this world.

"I think of Annie Sullivan. She was the ultimate cheerleader. She believed that anything was possible, and she did not stop communicating that belief, just because a

young woman named Helen Keller could not hear or see her. She forged a way to a bridge, simply tapping into a burning passion for letting every child know. Helen just got lucky. It was Annie's commitment."

-Sharon North Pohl

13. Lauren: I Can't Be Pregnant

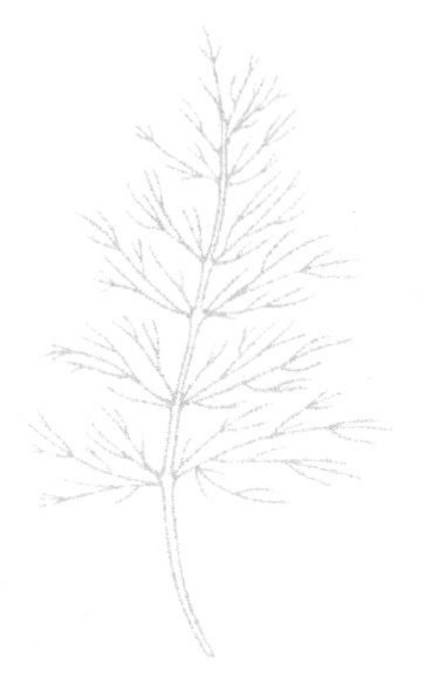

D i l l

"A woman is like a teabag; you never know how strong it is until it's in hot water."

-Eleanor Roosevelt

Hi, my name is Lauren Cohen. I am originally from Canada, and I live in South Florida. I am a corporate and immigration expert and a single mom.

When I turned 40, I had some major surgery. I was told I would never have children, and having children was the one thing I wanted most in the world. In fact, the second time I got married was pretty much so that I could have a child. In retrospect, thank God I didn't get pregnant!

Anyway, I had this major surgery. Doctors in two countries said, "No chance of getting pregnant, and if by some fluke, or a miracle, you get pregnant, you are never going to carry that pregnancy to term. It is not possible. Your body is a mess, and you will have a miscarriage."

At 42 years old, I went through the foster parent program to become a foster parent to kids in distress in South Florida. I took a foster baby home. He was four months old, and I was promised that he would be adoptable if the parental rights were terminated. If it weren't for that promise, I never would have taken him home, but of course, there are never any guarantees. I wanted very much to adopt a child. I didn't want to just continually foster, because I get attached.

Four days after I took that child home, I was pregnant. I didn't know it at the time, but I was. I did five pregnancy tests, lining them up on my counter. I had them from years of trying and never being successful. Every one of them said positive, and I still didn't believe it. I couldn't possibly be pregnant. I wasn't even really in a relationship at that time. I had resigned myself to the fact that I would be a mom to this foster child that would hopefully be adoptable.

That whole situation became extraordinarily complicated. I did not know I was pregnant until about two months in, so I had this foster child for about two months. I remember walking along the street and calling my dad, telling him I wasn't feeling well. He asked, "Well, what do you think it is?" I replied, "I don't know. Maybe I'm pregnant!" and started laughing.

I went to the doctor a few weeks later, and sure enough, I was pregnant. I remember being there with my friend, saying, "How is that even possible? I was told I couldn't get pregnant!" and then I got scared. Okay, I'm pregnant. Now what? I was afraid I wouldn't be able to carry this pregnancy to term.

I gave the foster child up to another family for short-term foster care. It turned out that for him, the parental rights were not going to be terminated. I had a very high-risk pregnancy, and I felt that it was some great miracle. I was determined to do everything in my power to make sure that the pregnancy was safe and carried to term.

My son is nine and a half, and I get tears in my eyes when I think of him. As much as he drives me crazy, he has completely changed my life. I feel that he is proof that miracles happen, and sometimes-or often-it's about your mindset. They say that a lot of people that adopt get pregnant right after adopting, and that's what happened to me.

My son is the light of my life. 90% of what I do, I do for him. He is an amazing child, my inspiration every day, and I'd like to inspire others to follow suit and have faith in their dreams and not just listen to what the doctors say. Sometimes there is a power greater than doctors that will dictate the way that your life goes.

I'm a single mom; it's never easy. I struggle. He's in a private school. It's challenging because I don't have a huge support network. I lost my dad six years ago, and my mom lives far away in Canada. But somehow, we've managed, and I wouldn't trade it for anything in the world.

If you have dreams of having a child, don't give them up simply because you are 40, or over 40. I'm 52 years old. He's nine and a half. And as I said, he is the inspiration for every day I live. Being a mom is the single most important job, or role, that I think anybody could ever have. I thank God for him every day.

"No one can truly explain "mind over matter", but it seems that intention really does play an important role in the body. When my intention is clear, my body responds with health and zest. When my intention is not clear, my body does not respond quite the same way. My intention is to be a big sister to the world. What is your intention?"

-Sharon North Pohl

14. Chineme: Whiplash

"You don't need proof when you have instinct."

-Quentin Tarantino

The day started off like any other. I happened to be driving to yet another tribunal hearing for one of my daughter's many due process cases.

I am a single mother and sole carer for my beautiful teenage daughter, who was born with a condition known as Williams Syndrome. People with WS have the cutest, pixie-like facial features, dazzlingly infectious smiles, and bright, chatty personalities, which tend to mask a multitude of physical, emotional, and cognitive issues.

From my daughter's birth, she was in and out of hospitals with various seemingly random conditions and high fevers, which were managed but remained unnamed, until she was over two and a half years old. Her diagnosis brought great relief, since putting a name to her condition meant that I could, at last, begin to deal with her varying symptoms with more precision.

However, along with that relief came what I can only refer to as sheer devastation, as it was finally confirmed that our lives were definitely not going to pan out in the general direction that I had initially envisaged, and indeed planned, for us.

It took a period of deep mourning for me to come to terms with the new direction of our lives, which I determined would nonetheless still be filled with fun and laughter. There would also be great difficulties, sadness, and isolation, along with a constant battle as I continue to advocate for my sweet pea through the myriad of medical, educational, social, and legal problems that she has required in order to be able to experience any semblance of a decent life.

There has never been any support provided by her biological father, or anyone else. As a result, we battle through the system and our lives by ourselves. Even the non-profit organizations and local government services were stretched so thin that they were utterly ineffective in carrying out their legal duties.

Our only support was the lifeline provided by my Dad, my daughter's granddaddy, who lived in a land far, far away. We spoke regularly on the telephone and visited once or twice a year until his devastating passing some years ago.

It was at that time that I really came to appreciate the true meaning, and the true feeling, of loneliness. Until then, my dad was the only one who took any interest in our day-to-day lives. He listened to our struggles while providing reassurance and much-appreciated advice and guidance.

My dad was the one who encouraged me to keep on fighting the good fight while celebrating every single one of our achievements, no matter how minuscule. He made us feel as though we were part of something more than the two of us. My dad was the one who shared our joy and laughter as though we were in the same room together. And then he was gone.

I was a senior corporate lawyer who chose to give up corporate life when my daughter was about 7 years old. It was not a difficult decision for me. I wanted to spend time - proper, quality time - with my child and ensure that I was there for all of her milestones, and of course, I was in a good position to advocate effectively for her many needs.

I started working from home as an online marketer. There were times when meeting the monthly outgoings was particularly challenging, but I loved every minute of my newfound freedom. Things were obviously still difficult, but while I was fit and healthy, we did okay.

So, back to that day that started off like any other...

I was driving through a highly congested Central London in wet conditions when I was suddenly shunted hard from behind by a London Taxi. The line of traffic was traveling no faster than 5 to 10 miles per hour, and the driver had tried to escape from the heavy traffic, only to be faced by oncoming traffic, which he then sought to avoid by veering straight into my car. I slammed on my brakes to avoid hitting the vehicle in front of me, pulled over, and got out of my car.

The taxi driver was very apologetic and immediately admitted liability for the accident. The impact had caused a painful twinge in my lower back and leg on the right side, but I was able to continue on my way after we exchanged details for insurance purposes.

However, as the afternoon wore on, I began to feel intense pain in my lower right back, shooting down the back of my leg. So severe was the pain that I had difficulty sitting. I went to the emergency room at the local hospital, with my daughter who had been returned from her school.

I became more and more distressed as the pain intensified; I had no idea what was happening and feared the worst. My worry was somewhat alleviated when the doctor explained that I had suffered from a whiplash injury. Apparently, whiplash is not limited to just the neck. Feeling relieved, I was given some strong painkillers and returned home.

By the next day, however, I had developed intense pain in my right arm and shoulder and could not use that hand. I went to my doctor and was told that it was the effect of the whiplash. They gave me another set of painkillers, and I went home. By that evening, my left arm and shoulder were affected in the same way, and from there began a nightmare of ailments affecting every joint in my body, first on one side, and then the other. Some days I was completely incapacitated and in intense pain, despite wolfing down an inordinate amount of prescription drugs.

It took almost a year of absolute torture before I got a firm diagnosis of Rheumatoid Arthritis. My RA had been triggered by the trauma of the whiplash, after which my anti-nuclear antibodies began to wreak havoc on my auto-immune system. It was during those dark days that it dawned on me just how vulnerable my daughter is when I cannot be my usual, active self.

I sank into a deep depression. Then, one morning, I forced myself out of bed and began to write. I reminded myself of how strong-minded I used to be, and I ended up writing a chapter of my first published book, *There Is No Time Like the Present to Create Your*

Future. It is a seven-step action plan for taking responsibility for one's well-being, creating a better tomorrow. Writing was a form of therapy. I recalled more energetic times, and, despite my continuing pain, I managed to use the power of my mind to dust myself off and begin again. After all, isn't that what I have always done? Absolutely, and I knew I could do it again. And I did.

A thought that has always made me laugh is, "You have one foot in the past, one foot in the future, and you are peeing on today". My future is here, now, because every investment I make in myself now arrives later in wellness. Every time I withhold from myself now? Yes, that also arrives later, just when I would have needed it...

-Sharon North Pohl

15. Esther: Sing Every Day

Basil

"The stars are always there, even in the daytime. Sometimes we just can't see them."

-Marian Keyes

Mrs. Hill was an African American woman who was our house cleaner. "Maid" is what they called it back then. Out of every person I've met in my life, she and my dad have been the biggest influences.

I was raised with an alcoholic mother who couldn't bear to be touched. The story is that I wasn't raised in love. But I did find the antidote. Whenever I have a significant challenge; life-threatening cancer, divorce, separation from a husband, and I don't know what will happen, I always return to my love of dance, nature, meditation, creativity, and friendship.

That combination, that antidote, they're my gems, they're my talismans, they're my way, my sense. On the outside, they are activities, but on the inside, it is returning to that innate wisdom that's within me, that experience, sometimes catalyst, for any particular meditation that I do. It can be picking up a book and getting inspiration from a phrase that reminds me of something I know on a deep level. The synchronicities that happen in my life are absolutely magical.

Once, as a child, they had me all dressed up in this fancy organdy dress. I got outside, and I wandered over to the next-door neighbor's apartment where there was a mulberry bush. I was gobbling mulberries and having a wonderful time...tie-dyeing my organdy dress without knowing it. Mrs. Hill came and found me, and she just laughed and said, "Oh, look what you've done! What are we going to do?" But it was with all this love, in contrast to fear like, "Oh my god, you're in the doghouse, you really screwed it up." She trotted me back home with this pure delight and love.

She had that kind of love and joy despite her own sufferings. I mean, my God, she had seven kids! Five days a week, after taking care of us all day, she would cook our dinner and then go home to deal with her own children.

I went away to college and didn't see her for a number of years. When I went to visit her, I just started weeping, and I had no idea why. That's when I realized how deeply I loved her. I had the epiphany of "oh my god, I'm never going to be separate from her again!" in the sense of losing touch, and I never did. I visited her up until she passed away at 101.

She engaged my ability to laugh in the midst of all kinds of crap going on. She assured me that everything would be alright, and again, we got to laugh together. That visit was the first reunion, and every time from then on, when we'd be together, we would laugh. As I write this, I'm crying because I realized that my gift for laughter came from Mrs. Hill.

Out of all that has helped me cope with everything, my most significant medicine has been the Gospel Choir I am in now. I always thought I couldn't sing, but I grew up with her spirituals because she sang all the time. I call on her every time before I sing in the choir.

As I go through my life and all the dark times, I know that there is this duality between the dark and the light. However, dark is what allows us to see the illumination from the other stars. Where I need an answer, I can always be patient and wait for the proper light. As Mrs. Hill used to say, "Child, the stars are only hidden by the daytime sun".

It's so funny; I needed so much to cry today.

I think we all happen upon a Mrs. Hill somewhere in our childhood. Who was your wise woman? Who gave you the tools to be the mentor you can be today? Who is learning from watching you, even now?

-Sharon North Pohl

16. Sonia: From the Mud Blooms the Lotus

"If you really want to do something you'll find a way. If you don't, you'll find an excuse."

– Jim Rohn

I'm a trader. I trade currencies using computer algorithms.

The turning point in my life came a couple of years ago, on my 50th birthday. Until then, I spent all my time looking after my family.

I have a daughter who is now 24 years old. She has an extremely rare illness. When she was diagnosed at four years old, there were only 30 people in the world that had it. For ten years, I was in and out of the hospital with her. There are now 127 people in the entire world with her condition. This is not about her, though; it is about me.

I basically spent all my time in and out of the hospital, and then I had to find another career. I was a very high-flying IT consultant on a huge salary. I had everything until I had my child. After that, I had to reinvent myself, and I did.

As a trader, I worked from home. I thought it was the ideal career for me because I could work around my child, as well as my parents, who had moved nearer to my house so I could keep an eye on them. I did everything for everybody else because that's how I was brought up. That was the era of bringing up girls to be great wives and great mothers. And yeah, there's something wrong with that. It's not everybody's dream.

While I don't regret anything, I do look back and think, "My God, how much time did I lose? I lost two decades. Two decades. I'm now 52; I'll be 53 in August." I say to myself and others, "I've got maybe 15 years of good health in front of me. I already have problems with my health; parts of my body are failing and don't work the way they used to.

I not only have 15 years of life to live, but I have the 20 years that I lost to make up. Basically I have 35 years of life to live, and 15 years to do it in." That is how I see it.

At 50, I turned myself into a social experiment. I said, "You know what, I'm just going to say yes to any opportunity that comes along and see what happens. Even if I don't know what to do, I will find a way to make it work."

I started to see more people getting out there. I realized I was losing social skills; I didn't perform well in large groups of people. I still don't. I get social anxiety quite a lot. I am okay one on one - I can talk for ages like I'm doing now. I had to do something. I had to create the avatar of the person that I wanted to be, and then find a way to be that person.

I'm not afraid of dying. If I die tomorrow, it won't bother me. What scares me is the idea of dying unfulfilled. That absolutely terrifies me; the thought that I lived and died and my life meant nothing because if I died today, everyone would get over it. There will be nothing to say that I ever existed. That pains me a lot.

I read a lot of books, not really self-development, but more about improving on who I am. I suppose that is self-development, but business skills and similar things as well. I read a fantastic book called *The Compound Effect,* about how all the small things you do end up being that massive thing. That was a big page-turner for me.

I joined a networking group in 2018. Again, I had so much social anxiety. When the mic came around for me to do my 30 seconds, my heart would be thumping. I would actually write my name down so that when I stood up, I would still remember it. That's how bad I was.

I kept on saying yes, kept on getting involved. Every time there was anything to do, I would go, and I would just volunteer. While sorting out tables or something, I'd be talking to people, connecting on various levels. I found that I can be quite good with people one on one, something I was unaware of. I would connect, and I would listen to their stories. I never talked about myself, always asked about you, who you are, what you're about, what do you want, how can I help you?

There would inevitably be some story to connect us, and that created more friendships and strengthened bonds. And I just found myself going from strength to strength.

Now, I am starting my own networking group. I have a nice little community. I've got women joining who have the same problem as me. More and more women are being drawn to me because they want to be where I am. I'm a speaker now, in my group. I'm not on the national stage or anything, but maybe I will be one day. I'm just going with the flow, but I love where I am.

Even this cruise that I'm on today, when my friend said, "Do you want to come?" I said, "You know what? Let's do it!" I came with no expectations. I met the most incredible people. I didn't come here for business; I just came here to see who else is out there. That was it. And I'm flying. I am absolutely flying.

I think my best years are actually in front of me, not behind me. Don't let age come into it. Don't let your health come into it. If you really want to do something, you will find a way. If you don't want to do it, you will find an excuse.

I always thought the power of purpose was this one massive thing that I had to do to make a big difference because you hear all the time, "Oh, I want to make a difference." I want to make a difference! I thought it was this big thing that I had to do, but it's not. It is all the small things that I had to do.

There's this lady that I knew in one of my groups, and she was in a very dark, dark place. She would come and talk to me every week. When she saw me, she'd come and talk to me, and I didn't really envision it because I'm not a coach or anything. I would just sit there and listen, and I would let her cry. She wanted to cry. Every time I wanted to say, "Look, we are here, whatever you need. We are here. Tell us what you need, and we will help you."

That woman is a completely different woman today. She's all, "Thank you, Sonia. Thank you, Sonia." She's won awards in our group and everything. We knew she was going to win, so we made sure she stayed. We paid for a ticket for her to be there so she would get her award, and she is walking on air now.

I see those things in people change, and I think, "Yeah, that's good." I had something to do with that. I got to be part of their journey. That makes me feel really good.

Tithing is not just for church, and it's not just a way to bring abundance. It's a thank you for what I have. When I give from abundance, no matter how little I have, somehow I attract a bigger flow of resources. So, what if you showing up for a friend or stranger is also tithing? Give and see.

-Sharon North Pohl

Rosemary

17. Janet: Downward Spiral

"Who said Been Down So Long It Looks Like Up to Me?"

-Richard Fariña

Wailing and flailing on the floor of my childhood bedroom, eyes locked on the round rug, I recall life is not linear. Now staring at the hardwood floors and stark white walls thru puffy eyes, I seek solace in my warm fuzzy clothes on my back.

It's daylight. Through blurry eyes, I notice the pink swirls on the white rug spiraling around me. I feel like I've been wrenching for hours, bawling my eyes out. My tongue feels like a toxic stew of trash coming out of my mouth. I recall life is not linear.

How did I get here? I don't want to think about it anymore. It's been days, or weeks, or longer...I'm so done with it! I'm done with everything. Where is my motivation to get off this floor - to go to the next floor... to do anything? I've known my purpose, igniting human potential, and I always thought that would be enough. But it is not. How can that not be enough? If it's true that it's not enough, what does that mean? What's next? Here I am, sick, years into adulthood, and on the floor of my childhood bedroom...and I don't know where I'm going to get the motivation to heal. And live.

Like a tube of toothpaste having its insides squeezed out, I surrender to this moment. I am humbled. Dear Life, "What?! What will motivate me to move forward, to heal, and be of service once again? Because at this juncture, I am done with life, yet I know the muted spark remains, so...what the fuck?!" I drop the question into an imaginary pink bubble on its way into the ethers. I go on with my days.

Days go by, and yet again, I'm on the floor. I don't want to be here, but this seems to be where the answers come. This is a safe place in some regards, and I have a roof over my head. In a state of curiosity and connection with the Universe, the answer whispers in my ear: CREATION. "What!? Creation? Ok, thanks, and SO WHAT?!, Now what?!" This abiding in the state of curiosity is working well, so I leave the question again.

After what feels like an exorbitant amount of time, the ethers finally nudged me with a pop-up command: *Take pictures of your emotions. All of them, not just the ones you like.* Happily, I obeyed this command and asked myself, "Janet, what does relief look like? What does compassion look like? And what does anger look like?" The closed bedroom door for privacy. Click. A selfie through the mirror, with me curling back my lips, squinting my eyes, scrunching my forehead. Click. This stupid overactive heater vent that won't close. Click. Clicking away, I notice a release of the heat from my veins. How does that happen with just three clicks with a smartphone camera?! This feels more like a choice than a "have to" be here, like a crack into freedom, an a-ha moment. I am CREATING with curiosity and a camera!

What a download from the Universe! This is going to prove to be a great gift; I can feel it. I suddenly recognized that I am Being WITH my emotions, in each moment, with each click! These energy forms that are meant to be simply observed, yet are typically met with resistance, now have NO power over me. I feel elated. I am entering sovereignty. I am reminding myself that E-motions are energy in motion and MUST move through us like a river or the wind. When I attempt to control them either by pushing away, changing, or attaching, I am creating blocks and scars in my energy body. Over time, these often have led to my conditioned fears, limiting beliefs, and a variety of illnesses.

I recognized the imperative of this process. It is my ticket to freedom from illness and limiting beliefs, holding me back from my potential. I thought, "Life, you are too funny!" just a few months after publishing my first book, *Me With Me,* I was being tested on self-love, self-care, self-honor. Ha! I am my first client!

The moment I decided to completely surrender into humility, at the most trying moment of my life, when I wanted to quit, I received that first process. I was down and out with adrenal exhaustion. It was a miracle response to a crucial need I had, the power of photographing emotions. My relationship with my emotions was a blockage. I had a need, found the solution, and made sacrifices to bring it to others.

I immediately noticed a reduction in depression, stress, and overwhelm, with a surge of vitality, personal power, and resilience. The more I practiced, the more my emotional blockages were released.

Over the next two years, I received two more significant messages from the Universe. The second was, using a camera, track subtle, evidence steps of my progress and wins. The third was, using a camera, capture the interpretation, opinion, or assumption that triggers my emotions in order to significantly reduce the emotional charge. I happily obeyed the instructions, which lead me to more ease, joy, and personal power. Ultimately, this 3-part process was my saving grace!

Fast forward to January 2020. After an in-home accident, I incurred a traumatic brain injury. By early March, I was DONE with life. I had no conviction to move forward with my healing. I saw no way out. Down in the depths of hell, having no answer to how I was going to make it through with all the medical expenses, rent, car, etc., whilst making zero dollars as a self-employed Life Transitions expert, I paused in sincere curiosity and asked Life, "What is option 3?!"

Did a concrete, obvious answer come? Nope. However, the action of ASKING THAT QUESTION was the magic. It put me in a place of 100% full acceptance of my situation. In that place, and ONLY with that attitude, could I hear the whispers, the answers to my problems.

The moral of the story is that favorable outcomes follow, to the degree you are abiding in sincere curiosity and to the corresponding degree to which fear is disempowered. Telling yourself the truth is easy by playfully abiding in sincere curiosity.

I'm happy to announce I am recovering well. All of my needs are met, such that I'm currently in the desert on my Soul-Tour, finally aligning all parts of me. Although I still have limitations, I have never felt freer or more sovereign!

Trust that life will give you exactly what you need, always and only just in the nick of time. That's why I always wait till the last minute before I figure out what to wear.

-Sharon North Pohl

18. Johanna: Art is My Path

Thyme

Happiness is not a matter of intensity but of balance, order, rhythm and harmony.

-Thomas Merton

I was a class clown, and I was hyperactive. School was never a challenge to me, so I was always first to finish my work. They were going to skip me a grade, but my mom asked them not to. She got skipped two grades in school, and it messed her up.

Basically, I was really intelligent, and I was dying for attention because I did not get any at home. I was a latchkey kid in Scotts Valley, California, and poor compared to everyone else I knew. We had chickens in the backyard. My mom was a high school teacher, and my dad got laid off from Seagate in the mid or late 90s, never going back to work. Life was pretty much "don't make trouble, don't ask for anything; basically, take care of yourself". I had a lonely, nature-filled childhood, and I was very insecure and very anxious.

I have since really strengthened my ability to be in the present. That has been healing, along with valuing my own health and well-being first. That's another thing I think we empaths tend to do—put other people ahead of ourselves. It gets you nowhere.

I used to be a river guide for whitewater rafting. When we did our first rescue training, I learned something that stayed with me and still pops back in my head: If you are trying to rescue someone, the first rule of rescue is to not become a victim. Do not put yourself in a bad way where you also, then, need rescuing.

That has been one of my mantras over the last few years. I really did put family, friends, and a lot of other things ahead of myself, but that leaves you depleted and is actually quite dangerous. I feel like I have a purpose and a mission now, however, and it is clear that I need to take optimal care of number one to be of any good to myself or anyone, and to do the work, make music, and make art. That has been a crucial lesson.

I had an unfortunate work experience about two, three years ago. It was a pretty traumatic harassment situation that forced me to change gears and finally ask for help, which was not a thing I ever did. It's sad; I ended up leaving that job because of it. It was the first time I ever took the physical steps to remove myself from harm, after taking all the proper actions but not at all getting the proper help.

I was working at a sports facility training in a sport that I love, and this person had been just one of the most unhappy people for the last few years before I ever met him. I'd been around him, and just seeing this person really sad and depressed, seemingly, I reached out at times as just a member of the community. We were co-workers, and came to be working closely in a few years after that. He was the type of guy who was obsessed with women, but had not had a genuine relationship, so they fantasize about certain women and become very attached. Our fellow co-workers all saw it.

One woman after another would disappear from the facility and wouldn't come back because of his unwanted attention. This guy also wasn't getting promoted, wasn't getting recognized by the company, wasn't moving up, and he really wanted all that. This added to the angst of the situation.

I started recognizing young women, who were maybe just barely of age, interacting with this predator in his mid to late 30s. Young women he was buying intimate gifts for. They'd say "so and so bought me this and that", and I would say, "Wow, okay, so are you one of the students? A friend?" And they say, "No, we just met."

For me, it reached critical mass when I sat through some horrendous mediations that were both traumatic and entirely ineffective. I have been a people pleaser my whole life, and I happened to be personal friends with both owners of this business. I don't know how it ever got to a point as bad as it got. I finally valued myself over the situation and the work, took all of my friends' advice and support, and left.

Being an introvert, I've been holding back on my art my whole life. I've been waiting for people to give me a leg up, help me somehow, or recognize something in me that I was disempowered to even like, share, or do anything about myself. That's how I really felt.

I used to not share anything. I recorded an album in 2009. I've probably written 60 plus songs, but maybe only 10 of those are recorded. I had a very harsh view and was very self-critical in general. After that experience, basically getting my soul tested along with my worth, my voice, and any agency of my own, I felt like I lost everything.

All I ever wanted and needed was a community. I truly felt like I lost touch because that guy was now slandering me, in my own community. I went into self-isolation for about a year and a half. I was tripping on the ego aspects of what people may or may not think of me, what they may or may not have heard about me, from this creepy guy who did his best to throw some serious shade at me.

This time put me in touch with my purpose. I had been walking around my whole life like I had an open wound, highly susceptible to all I hear and see and experience day to day. It has almost been too much, and it's taken a toll on me.

Still, through that experience of being pushed to the max and also having these really wonderful, steadfast friends who reflect back to me, I was finally made to accept my gifts, and that art is my path.

I delight in very average things, and I feel like it is my purpose to be a lens for other people and channel that in any way I can. I feel fortunate to have a skill set with a lot of different tools for doing that, so I have visual art, the music, and the writing itself without the music. It comes through me in different ways, by me being genuine, not judging my happiness.

During and since that experience, the gift of empathy at times has been painful. I feel lucky and fortunate that I haven't lost it. In fact, it seems to have actually increased since that experience.

I love it when I'm out in the world and have wonderful interactions with perfect strangers. Oftentimes they reflect back to me that they also really appreciated these interactions, and that it was something rare. I am just talking about those little conversations at the checkout. I didn't have a smartphone until about a year ago, so I'm the person sitting around making eye contact with people. I'm the one that's being present.

Is it OK to "unplug"? You'd damn well better once in a while! Oh, and check to make sure you were plugged in to begin with. Make sure you're not plugged up, or trying to plug a hole in yourself. Let it all go once in a while, laugh and skip and feel your beauty.

-Sharon North Pohl

19. Noel: King Lessons, cont.

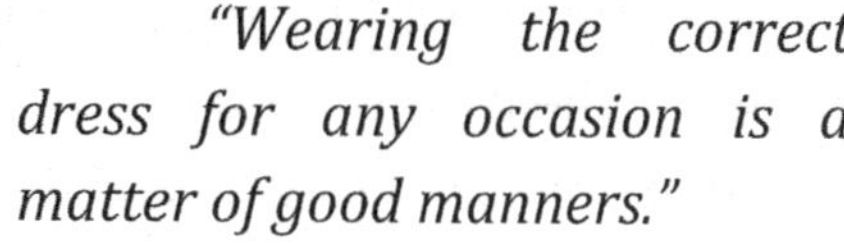

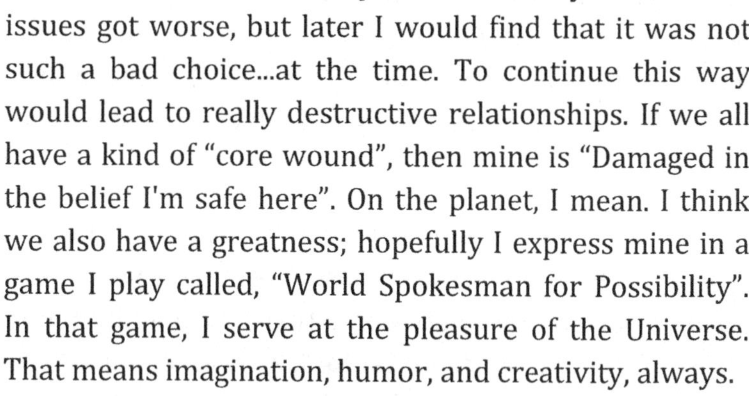

Arrowroot

"Wearing the correct dress for any occasion is a matter of good manners."

-Loretta Young

As a boy, I found an imaginary garment of steel and wrapped myself in it. My behavioral issues got worse, but later I would find that it was not such a bad choice...at the time. To continue this way would lead to really destructive relationships. If we all have a kind of "core wound", then mine is "Damaged in the belief I'm safe here". On the planet, I mean. I think we also have a greatness; hopefully I express mine in a game I play called, "World Spokesman for Possibility". In that game, I serve at the pleasure of the Universe. That means imagination, humor, and creativity, always.

I use something called NLP and EMDR to short circuit the terror I, even today, sometimes feel for no reason. When I am triggered, I stop breathing, and then I panic. Sometimes I don't realize that it has happened until later. I have been in situations where I was going to go on stage in front of thousands of people, and one foot or the other would cramp up like it was caught in a car door. I would saunter out on stage like a Zoot suit hipster to cover it. Once both feet cramped. That was an awkward entrance...

The panic I felt became like the noise of the city. If I go to the country, I'll need a tape of the city just to go to sleep. I was so used to it that I didn't even know I was slowly tearing down my adrenal glands. I experienced all this as an alcoholic teardown. As a professional comedian, I ran on nuclear energy, a steamroller.

Reasonable women bade well from afar, and I had a revolving door of insanity wrapped in its own steel. The women I attracted at that time in my life were, as it turned out, mostly survivors of sexual abuse, and I had no idea that the mutual wound was what brought us together. I was too closed to even get it.

When I was 30, the typical age of women I dated was 21, and I seemed immature to more than one of them. I wore tennis shoes and a tuxedo, sang Elton John and did jokes at a grand piano. I worked country bars with peanut shells on the floor. I played everywhere and slept in my car half the time. I was whoever you wanted me to be. Just don't ask me to be with me.

Once a guy was blocking the stage view with his cowboy hat. This spurred a fight; someone pulled a

Glock pistol and fired off 15 rounds. No one was hurt, but the gun guy escaped, and the cowboy hat guy lay on the hood of a car out front, sobbing uncontrollably. I was jealous of a man who could cry because I couldn't. Maybe if I were inches from death, I, too, could cry?

The next night I sang with a band for the Hell's Angels motorcycle brotherhood. Yep, someone touched a bike and got stabbed just outside the door.

I played gigs in comedy clubs, bowling alleys, even a nuns' fundraiser. In New York, I was doing four shows a night on the weekends, running a full-time comedy club in Manhattan, and I simply crashed.

Here comes the dressing up part. I was broken open, and what came out was pure pain. A hurt locker of my own. My personality in its entirety was built up as a main defense against anyone getting in... ever.

Today I am 35 years without a drink. My cat has never seen me drunk (she is 22). I was confronted about my pattern of attracting abused women by being told that, in order to attract that, there must be something inside of me. How could I know? I couldn't feel any emotions other than anger and, well, nothing. Numb...

Years ago, I was on a radio show with a group of women. They agreed that these abuse issues were not understandable to men. I choked. My response was that so many men had untreated sexual abuse issues that it was driving a stake into the lives of good dads and husbands, ripping families apart. One responded to me "well, at least they don't have body issues like we do".

The truth is that body shame from sexual abuse is rampant among men as well. We simply don't discuss it, ever. The first rule of fight club is never talk about fight club. Oh, me? Yeah, I'm a renegade.

I've traveled the western US as a keynote speaker for the Salvation Army, saying exactly this to 300 men at a time. They, too, were dressed for battle at a garden party. I've done sober conventions, spoken at high school graduations, but I still can't talk about it one on one. That is still too vulnerable.

I dressed for battle when my heart wanted to go barefoot. I did every workshop, therapy, got certifications, and tore at my defenses. I committed to things that required my heart, knowing I could at least confront it. I had dressed myself so tightly in steel and weaponry that I couldn't get out. The way I dress for competition is shorts and Ugg boots. I have tailored suits for business, and orange, yellow, and purple suits (even tuxedo tails) for onstage.

When grief is up, dress it in swaddling clothes. When celebration comes up, dress it in joy. When a challenge arrives, dress it in conviction. When it's time to love, dress it in your zest.

-Sharon North Pohl

20. Sharon: The Baby Comes

Lemon Zest

"You must do the things you think you cannot do."

– Eleanor Roosevelt

I left Hawaii behind me and headed for rainy Oregon. I went to my sister's house, where my sister and her husband welcomed me with open arms. That was truly lifesaving after my parents' rejection. I was empty, no money, no happiness, and very little heart for life. My parents wanted nothing to do with me, and I was deeply hurt.

I was angry at such a deep level at Gary for terrifying me, threatening my life, and putting me in the situation. I cycled between grief and anger at a dizzying speed. I could barely sleep or eat, but I knew I had to keep nourishing the life growing inside me. I was in a state of total depression and confusion as to what to do next. I had to figure out a way to stay sane and focus on what to do. I came up with a plan that has served me then and for the rest of my life.

I decided to get out, to go outside every day, and start walking—the time I spent outside helped me find some peace of mind. I was hopeful that the exercise and contemplation might give me back the ability to sleep at night. I began using the walks as a kind of ambulatory meditation. I started noticing things around me and paid attention to my five senses: Sight, Sound, Smell, Taste, and Feel. I admired the beautiful gardens, their bright colors, and the smell of the flowers. I heard the birds and observed their different calls and songs. I noticed the feel of the breeze on my skin, the smell of the rain.

Slowly these walks started to help me out of my self-pity and debilitating anger. I was alive! I was ready to rejoin life. I gained the strength to start figuring out what I would do next. Getting out mobilized me, got me out of bed and back into the world.

That daily discipline was one of the most important discoveries of my life. Getting out into nature, even if it is just in your own neighborhood, can totally disrupt self-defeating, unhealthy thinking. It is a type of being in the here-and-now walking meditation.

I knew I had to make a birth and adoption plan soon. I was 7+ months along. I could no longer be in denial of the inevitable. This baby would be born. I did not believe I had the resources, financially or mentally, to go it alone, raising a child. I was terrified of Gary, afraid for my life and the safety of my baby. I didn't have the money to go to a private obstetrician.

I researched and found an adoption agency in Portland, the Boys and Girls Aid Society. They set up an appointment with a county-paid doctor, the kind provided in welfare cases. I met with the social worker and gave her the intake information. The thinking of the day was to encourage all unwed mothers to give up their babies for adoption. I gave them information about my family medical history. I gave them the name of the father, wrote about the type of family I was hoping would adopt my baby, and believed in my heart of hearts that a stable married couple would be the best. This was something that I could not provide.

By October, I hadn't made it to my first appointment yet. They were really busy, and after all, I was only seven and a half months pregnant. On October 14, 1968, I went for my longest walk ever, and when I got home, my water broke. Neither my sister nor I could believe it because it was too soon. My sister took me to the county hospital, and by then, I was in full-blown labor. It was too late to stop it, even though the timing would make the baby six weeks early.

I was in a county hospital full of indigent women in a ward filled with prostitutes, drug addicts, and mentally ill women. It was the most demeaning experience of my life. My baby girl came into the world that day, October 14, 1968. The agency's policy was for me to not see or touch the baby for fear that I might change my mind. They had already chosen an adoptive family. In 1968 the culture was not accepting of unwed mothers raising their children. I walked by the nursery every day I was in the hospital, guessing which baby girl might be mine. I would stand at the nursery window and look in the incubators because my baby was six weeks early. She was tiny, just over 4 pounds.

I couldn't stand the pain. I left the hospital as soon as possible, leaving that awful ward behind me, and putting this part of my life in the past. The sadness I felt leaving that little girl behind burned deep in my soul. Her birth certificate called her baby girl Polland. I named her Ellianna that day. In my world, she always had that name. I would think of her every day for the rest of my life, and I would think of her as Ellie.

When I walked out of that place, I had hit rock bottom. I knew that no matter what happened in my life from here on out, nothing would be as bad as this gut-wrenching pain of leaving the blood of my blood and the bone of my bone behind. I was devastated, and the separation anxiety was huge. The sadness I felt was incapacitating.

The experience of being an unwed mother completely disrupted any plans I had for the future. I didn't go back to college in earnest until years later, and I never did graduate. I sold my car and what was left of my belongings and bought a ticket to London. I spent the next year wandering about Europe, looking for solace in the exotic and unfamiliar places, trying to bury my grief and shame.

-Sharon North Pohl

PART 3: GET OUT

"I raise up my voice—not so I can shout but so that those without a voice can be heard."

—Malala Yousafsai

Get Your Free Guide

Scan the QR code to get free tips, recipes, and guides.
www.zestychange.com/guide

21. Fran: World Record Mindset

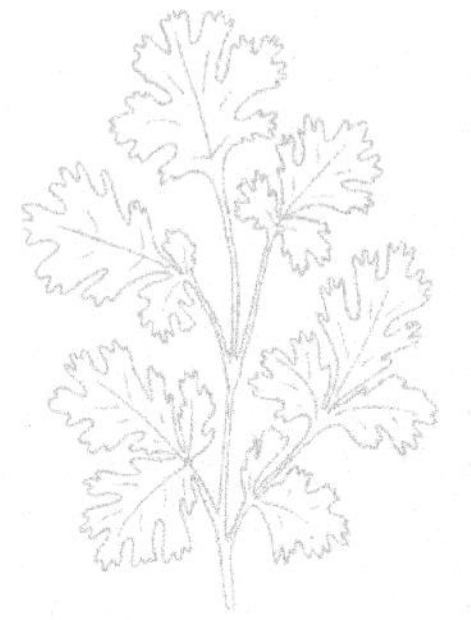

Cilantro

"The limits of the possible can only be defined by going beyond them into the impossible."

-Arthur C. Clarke

I'm usually of the mindset “Hey, I'll get over it.” I allow myself to feel the emotions, and then I go through it, whatever “it” is. I have been held up at gunpoint twice, had my house burned down. I took care of both my parents during cancer. I’ve been through some stuff!

I was working at a copy shop in Queens. It was the end of the night, I was there by myself, and these two guys came in, all rushed. They asked for business card samples, and when I turned around, they pulled their guns on me and demanded the money in the drawer.

Angry that the drawer contained only twenty bucks or so (I’m not sure what they expected, copies were 5 cents apiece...), they took the gold necklace I was wearing, and one guy told me to go in the back room.

He said, "Count to 100! If you come out before you count to 100, we're going to shoot you." I said to myself, "Okay, I'm going to go in the back room," and then I started thinking, "I'm the world's fastest talking woman. I'm going to count to 100, that will take all of a second!" So I went in the back, realized that there was a phone, and called 911.

The police showed up, and obviously, the guys had run away. A policeman asked me, "How come you're not crying?" I said, "Because I'm not dead." He continued, "No, but seriously, most people who get held up would be crying if they were by themselves." I responded, "I don't know what to tell you. I'm not dead, so that's why I'm not crying. Of course, if I was dead, I couldn't cry, so either way." Then he asked, "Were you in on it?" I said, "Seriously, for 20 bucks? No, I don't think so."

I mentioned I'm the world's fastest talking woman. I have seven other world records, none of which I had planned to do in advance. I have what's called a "World Record Mindset." An opportunity presents itself, and because I have the mindset of "Just say yes, and figure it out later," whenever something comes up, I do it.

It started with the fast-talking. People would always tell me I talk fast. I decided, "Okay, you know what? I'll do that!" I called up Guinness and asked, "What do you have to do to break the record?" They said something from Shakespeare or the Bible. Well, me and Shakespeare never got along, but I had a prayer from the Bible.

I decided to call the lady at six o'clock. She printed it on paper, and the very next day, the Larry King Live people called me up and asked me to go on the show and break the record. I didn't know who Larry King was. I asked, "Is this some kind of porn?" They said, "Oh, honey, no, it's a national show!" I said, "Well, what if I don't break the record?" "Larry doesn't care whether you break it or not. He just cares that you try it on his show first." I figured, what's the worst that can happen? I look like a fool on national TV. What's the best that can happen? I break a world record.

I went with that philosophy of "Just say yes and figure it out later." I went on the show and broke the record at that time, doing 585 words a minute. I re-broke it again at the Guinness Museum in Vegas, at 602.32 words a minute. That's 11 words a second.

I have this passion for life, everything. I see something, "Oh, that guy runs a marathon. I could run a marathon! That guy writes a book. I could write a book!" That's how I have written 22 books.

The next world record came about when I was working on a book called *Adrenaline Adventures.* I wanted to verify that this rock-climbing adventure still existed, so I called up the company. I asked if they still did rock climbing, and they said, "Not only that, we also climb mountains". He mentioned mountains I hadn't heard of and then asked, "Would you climb Mount Kilimanjaro?" I said, "I don't know. Let me look it up."

I discovered that an 83-year-old woman had climbed Kilimanjaro. I figured that meant I could do it. It wasn't until later that I found out she was airlifted... Nevertheless, I trained with my son, and we climbed it. We had minus 15 degrees with 45 miles an hour wind.

I wanted to do something more than just get to the top, so I brought books with me and became the first author to do a book signing at the top of Kilimanjaro. I also did a book signing down by the wreck site of the Titanic. I went with 29 chiropractors to the Dominican Republic, and we saw 21,695 patients in two days. I ziplined inside an active volcano in Nicaragua.

Recently, I did my first TEDx talk. When I was rehearsing, the producers said, "Can you try to break a record on the stage?" I'm like, "What? A TEDx talk isn't enough?" I did my entire 18-minute TEDx talk, and then I redid the talk in under a minute.

I have a one-woman show called *Love, Laughter, and Light,* which combines my standup comedy, motivational speaking, and wild adventures. I love motivating people by telling them how mindsets enabled me to accomplish eight World Records. My story wound up appearing in Chicken Soup for the Woman's Soul.

I would do it at 20, I would do it at 90, it doesn't matter. That's the thing, I have a very young mindset. Because of that, I don't want to be pegged in any category. I say "37 till I'm 97" because a scientific experiment showed that when people don't focus on their age and don't repeat their age, they actually live in the age that they believe. I'm like, "Well, good, then I'm living at 37."

That's pretty much how it is. I see friends my same age, and they're like, "Fran, we can't do that because we're..." I go, "Okay, you can't do that. I don't know how you got old. I didn't get old. I'm still 37," and that's always how I keep it. Stop with the label, stop with the restrictions. There is nothing except what your mind believes you can do. That's it. Jack LaLanne for God's sake! I don't remember how old he was at whatever point, but he was pulling boats with his teeth at 80 years old!

Stop it already with this "you can't do this at a certain age". You could do anything.

I look back to when Helen Reddy sang "I Am Woman". It was at a time when equal rights for women did not pass as law. It was a song about who you could be. Today, and even after hearing it sung by drunken men at karaoke nights, I see it's really my song too. I look back at my accomplishments, and I see that when I express my talents and gifts, it lights the path for others, and I also know my sisters are watching and following. When I dare to wear a crown and dress in flowing colors, they sometimes pick up my vibe, and I get to see flowers blooming in their eyes.

-Sharon North Pohl

22. Dee A: Never Really the Hero

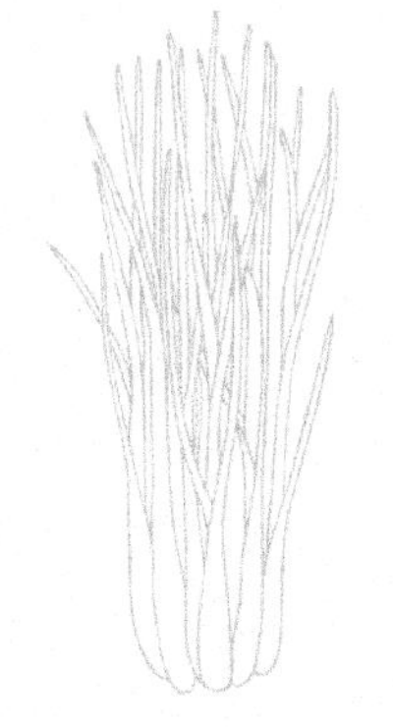
Lemongrass

"Every father should remember one day his children will follow his example, not his advice."

– Unknown

I grew up in active addiction; basically, I was born loaded. I always say my amniotic fluid was red wine.

I know people laugh. They think it's really funny. It was not funny then. It is pretty funny now because, really, that's how it was. My mom drank a box of wine a night, my dad drank a case of beer a day, so how could I not have gotten this thing called addiction and alcoholism?

Not only that, but the biggest way my parents showed love was with food. Hello, eating disorder! From the time I was four or five years old, our signature dessert before bed was booze and ice cream. I don't know if they just didn't read past "chocolate" on the chocolate coffee liqueur, but I got as much as I wanted almost every night, with ice cream.

I was born in the summer of 1969 into a "his, mine, and ours" family. When my parents got together, my dad had three kids, my mom had one, and then together, they had me. My closest sibling is nine years my senior; there wasn't much family bonding or connection. There was, however, a lot of dysfunction. My parents were both active alcoholics and raised me in a state of chaos. I never really felt safe, and I didn't get along with any of my siblings. There was a lot of disease in the home, lots of yelling.

My sister had my mom's insanity. My sister and my dad were at each other's throats, and he got physical with her. By late middle school, I was the only child at home, which made me effectively an only child. I was as close to my parents as one could be, in the midst of that chaos and that swirl.

Drug-wise, I was doing more food than anything until I started drinking more seriously in early high school. I was working with my dad and stopped for beers after work with him. I remember going to the local bar where he worked, and it was no big deal for me at 17-18 years old to be sitting there at the bar with his group of friends, shooting the shit and pounding down Miller High Life. They were super cold, ice on the bottles, and it was just what my dad did.

To get my first car, I got my dad drunk. We stopped at the car dealer on the way home, and I got a Camaro Berlinetta. I was like, "Just sign here," and he signed. That was kind of what I knew. I started with that manipulation early, knowing how to get what I wanted from my parents.

My dad always had hidden money. He kept it under the floor mat in his car. He got two separate checks from work. Whenever I needed money, whenever I needed anything, I had a full stash of cash.

The dysfunction of my mom and dad was intense. It was usually pretty quiet until they were both loaded and it was time to go to bed. Or, my mom would try to control my dad's drinking, and he would spout off when he finally couldn't stand it anymore. Then I was the peacemaker; I was the baby. Half the time, I was the scapegoat. I was never really the hero; that was my sister.

Sometimes, I would protect my mom when my dad started to get angry. There was never any physical violence between the two of them. It was always verbal. My room shared a wall with theirs, so I always heard everything. Five nights a week, I went to bed crying myself to sleep.

My drinking escalated once I could go out to the bars. I was on dart leagues; we would go shoot pool, and

I was out till one to three o'clock in the morning. I was trying to go to work at five or six. It just obviously took a turn for the worse.

In the midst of that, I had become friends with my ex. He ended up rescuing me from all of my situations. I would be at someone's house, and he would come get me. I'd be at the bar, unable to drive; he'd come to pick me up. I'd be at some guy's house; he'd come get me. I would call him and say, "I probably shouldn't drive," and he'd be like, "Don't move, I'll come get you."

I think that went on for six to eight months. I didn't have a long drinking career, because I went so hard, so fast, so heavy, and I was really young. I was 22 and didn't know any other behavior. I never really had people over. When I would go to a friend's house, it was like I was in the twilight zone, and when I met my ex, I was over there for family dinners. They literally sang Kumbaya.

They were in recovery themselves; they were vegan. I came from mashed potatoes, butter, gravy, bologna, fried chicken, and smoking... it was so bad, the smoke, that it was dripping down the wallpaper. I never understood what it was, but the tar was literally dripping down the appliances in our kitchen from the sheer amount of smoke. My dad smoked Lucky Strikes, and my mom smoked Viceroys.

My ex's mom is the one that helped me get into treatment. She's a therapist, as is his stepdad. We had a powwow on a Saturday morning, and Thursday, I was headed to Florida for an eating disorder and alcoholism.

Today I work in addiction treatment medicine. I have built and opened treatment centers. I have a private practice. I am doing a lot of work with firefighters and first responders. It truly is my life's work because I feel like I have been there and have come out on the other side.

When I started working, I showed up every day for about three months past my internship. I made friends with everybody that worked there, including the lady that finally hired me. I started out doing what is called chemical dependency evaluations, basically placement for level of care, and trying to filter the clients into our program, or whatever program they were willing to do that was a good fit.

My first evaluation was on the adolescent unit. As we walked in, she handed me the chart and said, "It's all yours." I opened the chart to the first sentence of the history and physical of what brought the kid in. He was 11 years old. I closed the chart, and I said, "Boss, I am really sorry, I can't do this. I don't know what I was thinking." She said, "What do you mean? I hired you because I believe in you, and I know that you can do this."

We talked for a few minutes, and she said, "Just go be you. You know, you're the first one to say add more love, love the people, love the client, regardless of how they show up." I said, "Sheila, this kid's 11 years old. What does he know about trying to hang himself?" She said, "Well, you are going to find out." I thought, "I can love this kid. I can go in there, and I can hopefully shift his perspective."

When we finished, he gave me a hug. I told him, "You know, regardless of what you think or how you feel, you are loved, you are worthy, and I, for one, will love you until you love yourself." This is my constant mantra with my clients—that I am going to be here, and I am going to deeply love them until they can love themselves. I believe that love can heal almost anything, and that is when everything changes.

When somebody can show up and say they love you and have it be unconditional, even though you relapse, even though you didn't do your assignments, even though you're not going to meetings, that, I think, matters. I tell my clients all the time, "I love you." I believe so many of us come from that space of not feeling loved, of that disconnection from our family.

I love unconditionally. That doesn't mean you get to treat me like shit, and I'll love you anyway. It just means that regardless of where you're at, I think love heals anything. For most people with addiction and substance use disorders, it all goes back to trauma, attachment, abandonment, neglect. If they feel that love from me, it may be something they've never felt before. The kids at the camp used to tell me that I was the mom they always wish they had.

I believe my superpower is love. I have it tattooed on my arm. It's one of my favorite hashtags (*#morelove*) because I could know everything in every single book, and I could quote the big book of AA, but if that person in front of me doesn't feel like they are loved, that I care about them, and that I'm there 100% for them, I could know everything, and it's not going to matter.

I am really good at helping to inspire people to see what's possible. In April, I have 29 years sober, and I have worked in the field for about 25. It is my absolute greatest joy. I have never felt burned out. I am excited to go to work every day because it doesn't feel like work to me. I get to carry that message, and be that light and the change that I feel people need.

I, too, can be very heroic. I am a hero to my future self by self-care now. My future self is heroic, too. She is kind to me when she has to finish the stuff I forget to finish. She's even kinder when I leave a mess for her to clean up later. However, I have found that she has her limits. Some days I clean up a little bit more and am a little bit more aware, so I really do live into my vision for myself. Those are the days I'm all the hero I need. After that, when I hear a man's voice speak the invitation to be small so he can rescue me later, I don't seem to hear it quite as piercingly. I am all the hero I need just for today.

-Sharon North Pohl

23. Gini: True Power

Sage

"Forgiveness is the greatest gift you can give yourself. It's not for the other person."

-Maya Angelou

I was born to very, very rich parents. My brothers and sisters were all older than me, and they received all the benefits of wealth: traveling the world, et cetera. However, fairly soon after I was born, my parents divorced. I was a premature baby. My mom and I never really bonded because I was in an incubator.

My mom got into heavy drug addiction, so my dad got custody of me. He was big on me having a relationship with my mom. The problem with that was that she was pretty far down the hole. We had a nanny who refused to take me to my mother's house because it was so full of drugs, drug dealers, and crazy people. My dad fired her, essentially because she refused to take me there.

When I was in fourth grade, my mom got arrested with me in the car. Everybody in the car was high. First of all, she took me out of school – she wasn't supposed to take me out of school. Then she and her friends were getting high in the car, driving around town. They got pulled over. My mom was using a fake ID, and the cop showed me the ID and asked, "Is this your mother?" As an 11-year-old, I had to say, "no, that's not my mother", knowing that he would arrest her.

He arrested her and left me with this drug dealer, one of the most sadistic people that mom had ever known. That was the option though, they could either take me to juvenile hall and have my dad and my stepmom pick me up, or they could leave me with this guy.

I stayed with him for a day, for 24 hours, because they figured if they could make bail for my mom, then no one would ever have to know that this happened. I finally demanded that he take me home to my stepmother, which he did.

This kind of cycle with my mom went on throughout my life as she spiraled further out of control. In high school, I was living in Colorado with my sister and my stepmother, and I came home to Houston for the holidays. My mom, who at this point had been arrested by the FBI and the Secret Service for identity theft, decided that we were going out to dinner.

She picked up a gun and put it in her purse, and I thought, why do we need that? It was pretty scary. I called my boyfriend and told him he had to come to pick me up because I wasn't going to be around somebody in a situation where we needed a gun. People were out to get her for having ratted them out.

My mom wound up going to prison for three and a half years. When she was incarcerated, I pretty much decided that I never wanted to have a relationship with her again. It had been too painful, too many abandonments, too many times where my mom would put my life in danger.

In prison, she met a man who was a pastor. They wound up getting married, and when she got out, they began working on me to try to have a relationship with her again. I was adamantly against it. I was like, "I don't need her. I lived my whole life effectively without her. Except for the time that she was behind bars, she's only brought me pain."

But eventually, I decided to just give it a chance. I made up my mind to forgive her and to see what would happen. The way I thought about it was, "What do I have to lose? I have already, in my heart, said goodbye to this relationship, so what do I have to lose? If I just try to forget, what would that look like? I have been through all this pain already; I know that I can survive that, so why not take forgiveness for a spin?"

I ended up forgiving my mother. Together, she and I went on this journey of her being accepting of everything that she had done, really laying everything out and examining it, and me forgiving her for those things.

Down the line, my mom and I even built a business together. We live next door to each other, and we have this fantastic relationship that we would never have had, had I not been able to forgive. I could have easily walked away from it, right?

My mom wasn't there for the first half of my life, but she is here now, for the second half. We've built amazing things together, spoken across the country, bringing our story to people, showing them what there is to gain if you can kick drugs and alcohol, along with showing people that forgiveness is possible.

It is like this gift that you give yourself. That sounds corny, but it's true. When you forgive, you have to stop holding those things against that person. I feel, in my heart, that I have transformed that anger into just understanding. She had so much pain and so many things that caused the drug addiction, and I have so much compassion for that. Forgiveness has helped me turn that into compassion for the person that she was.

We are all just doing the best that we can with what we have at any given moment. I am so grateful that I forgave my mother and that she has forgiven herself. There are some days where it is harder for her to forgive herself, but she works on it all the time. We truly have this fantastic relationship. We have built amazing things together, and the fact of the matter is that none of that would have ever happened without forgiveness.

If I want to forgive someone, it's a good idea to first make sure it actually happened. It's awful to forgive someone when they didn't do anything. Forgive my intrusion...

-Sharon North Pohl

24. Pam: Know When to Fold 'em

Marjoram

"There is no greater agony than bearing an untold story inside you."

-Maya Angelou

I have lived across three continents. I was born in India, moved to the UK in 1967, and lived there for 24 years. After I got married, we moved to Kenya and lived in Africa for 20 years. Being a qualified chartered accountant, having been brought up and educated in the UK, I was surprised to find myself in a very abusive marriage.

I moved to Kenya trusting my husband, never having been to the country. Life there was really hard, and I was quite suicidal at times. I fell pregnant within a few months of arriving in Kenya, and I had one child already. It's very difficult to leave a marriage as such, so I decided to stay for the sake of the children.

Things got steadily worse financially and emotionally, but I didn't know the word abuse. I bottled everything up and didn't tell anybody how I felt, and because of that, I started to get sick in very physical ways. I've had 3 D&Cs of the uterus, a lot of skin disease, fainting, blackouts. Now, in hindsight, I know that it was all internalization, and it's the body's way of ridding itself of what is toxic.

As I mentioned, I stayed because of the kids. I also left because of the kids. My oldest was 16, and the youngest was 12. He could hear all the shouting and fighting that was happening in the bedroom. He is a bright kid, a star, top in drama, top in sports, everything. One day, the headmaster called me into his office and said, "Jus is behaving in a strange way. He's throwing things at the teacher. When the girls walk past, he's calling them names in public." I was like, "That doesn't sound like anything like my son." Then I put that together with what was happening at home.

He was 12 years old, and he had started to cut up sheets and shower curtains. He had taken matches, and he started to burn the computer covers and things like that. When I finally put two and two together, I realized the traumatic effect our situation had on him.

Six months before that, I had just started my own business. I landed the largest contract in Africa. Then came the choice, do I stay there and grow this huge business that has landed in my lap, a business I have worked hard for and scaled myself up for, or do I take care of my kids? It was a no-brainer. The decision was, "I'm going back to the UK. Enough is enough." I told my husband, "I'm going to move back to the UK." Obviously, he didn't want me to. He said, "Oh, please stay one more year." I said, "No." I'm so glad I did.

They say in an abusive marriage, leaving is not the hard part; not going back is. On average, a woman leaves her husband seven times. I thought life would be easier once I got back to the UK, but it was worse. My husband had said, "You know what? Go back to the UK but say you're going for the children's education". I would have done anything to get away, so I agreed.

I moved to the UK "for the children's education," but really close friends realized that something wasn't right. Now, my husband is very mild-mannered. I'm very bubbly. When I got to the UK, I stayed for one week with my best friend. I used to go back every year, but on those trips, I never told a soul what I was going through. This time I stayed with her, and for a week, like vomit, it just poured out of me. It took a whole week to go through what I was going through.

My best friend, her husband, myself, and my husband all went to the same university, so they knew him very well ever since those years. They couldn't put it together, and they said, "You know what, Pam, we can't help you. This is such a serious kind of thing. You need to tell his family."

He has cousins who are quite dominant. We decided to go tell the cousins. My friend came with me, we told them, and they were gob smacked. They could not believe what was happening, but they also knew me; they knew how hard I had worked in their family business and the sheer amount of charity work I had done.

They wanted his side of the story, so they flew my husband in and said, "What is this? What's happening?". My friend, my sister, and his cousins essentially sat him down in a room, and he burst into tears and played the victim, "Pam doesn't let me watch TV..."

My friend came up to me and said, "What have you done to your husband?" "What?! I'm the one he beat physically...I'm the one he slapped and said, 'Don't forget you are no more than the boss's wife.'"

Now there were two very different stories. That's why I said it got worse, because now that it was out in the open, they are a well-to-do family with a reputation to protect, so they wanted me to take the tumble. I had them picking on me. When you haven't done anything, when you've struggled, and you've kept the peace, to be picked on like that I felt was worse than the abuse. They wrote an eight-page separation document, and how they managed to make him look a hero was, I think, one of the most hurtful things.

Anyway, I wondered as an educated girl, what the hell happened? How did I end up here? Why did I behave this way? Why did I stay in an abusive marriage? I believe it was in part because I grew up watching my dad slap my mom around. Some way, subconsciously, you then think that behavior is ok. Even when I told my mom and dad, my mom, because she had grown up with it, said, "Oh, so he slapped you a few times, why don't you go back?"

I needed to learn more about how this could have happened to me. I googled 'jealous, possessive husband.'

The word abuse came up, and I googled more, and this book kept coming up. It was *"Why Does He Do That? Inside the Mind of an Angry Controlling Man"* by Lundy Bancroft. I ordered it from Amazon. I read it, took a pencil, and started to underline. I underlined more than half the book because it was like writing a diary, the stages that happen in a marriage, the different types of abuse. It was the biggest eye-opener, and the book said, "Go to counseling."

What made me turn my life around was counseling and NLP. I became an NLP practitioner, and then I became an NLP master practitioner. I wanted to learn why I stayed, what happened, why people behave the way they do.

For me, that power was the knowledge that it wasn't my fault but also accepting that things are in my control. It was my fault. When you are controlled, you must admit that you let yourself be controlled, be it, say, for the children...

The biggest lesson on the zest for life is, "You know what? You have a choice. You actually do have a choice". I know it is really complicated when you're in a difficult marriage. When you've got children, you wonder how you are going to manage, practically and financially. How??

But staying in an abusive marriage and getting sick is not a life. You are dying inside. It's just not a life. I would tell anybody in an abusive relationship to get help. Just get help. Having that somebody talk to you, somebody who's been through it, counseling groups, anything, just get yourself some help and then move on—and do it slowly. I took counseling for four years. It took me six, seven years to wind down my Kenya businesses, but I've started new businesses and now look at me, I'm out marketing, out meeting people.

I've met the most amazing people since I've come out here. It is hard to start a new life at this age, after 50. But, boy, is it possible, and boy is it worth it. I'd say to all women out there who are going through it, just get help. You are not alone. That's the most important thing.

"Sometimes, the hardest choice you have to make is the one that's best for no one but you. Feelings will be hurt, but your wellbeing matters. You have a life to live."

-Sharon North Pohl

25. Lynn Ruth: My Comic Radiance

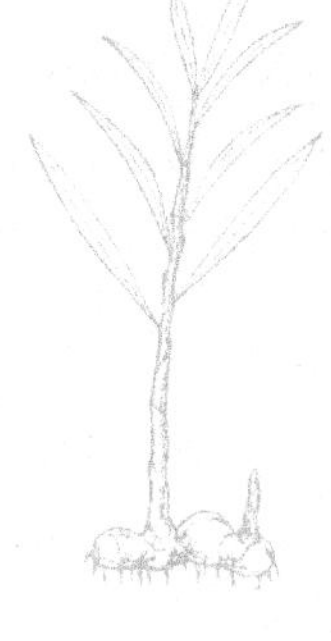
Ginger

"You are never too old to set another goal or to dream a new dream."

-C.S. Lewis

I am trying to change the world. I want people who are 60 and older, getting to the end of their first career, to reinvent themselves with a second career. It doesn't have to be a money-making career, but something new and different that is all their own because they have 20 years of marvelous health ahead of them. They know who they are, their financial status is set, and whether it's good or bad, they're used to it by then.

We can do incredible things, for humanity, for the world, and for ourselves, but some of us don't because we are not aware of our options. Many options are closed to us, simply because we're old.

I am trying to prove that life is good, and life gets better every year. I'm 86, and I am fighting ageism, I'm fighting sexism, I'm fighting misogyny. I'm fighting for diversity. I'm fighting for people to discover their inner potential. I am saying that when you are younger, you are too busy earning a living and bringing up a family to really know what that potential is, but when you get to be in your 60s, you have a pretty good idea.

I am now 86, and I am on my way. I'm not done by a long shot. I have a great deal more to do with my life. Please, God, I hope I can.

I was born in the 30s, so I was taught that nice girls get married and have babies. I got a beautiful education at the University of Michigan, which at that time was very much like Berkeley in California, very Avant-Garde. I was surrounded by people where education really mattered, where stereotypes were in the process of being destroyed. I was into a very liberal, open way of thinking. When I got out of school, I found out that the rest of the world didn't think that way.

I got married, got a degree in education, and taught school. I taught in Cleveland two years later, after I put my husband through Harvard Business School, and then made a mess of that. I was on my own again.

I started a TV program on CBS, a public service TV program for children because my master's degree by that time was in creative arts for children. And I was divorced. In those days, 1958-1959, divorce was a sin. I was the first person in my family to divorce. I was not particularly a feminist; I was somebody trying to make it with all the cards stacked against her.

Since the TV program was a public service, I was not paid. It went on for two years. I stopped teaching during that time and became my father's secretary. What I ended up doing was watering plants. In those days, the only jobs that women didn't have to fight, scream, and claw their way into were secretary, schoolteacher, housewife, or prostitute. All of which amount to serving men.

I was my father's secretary, I was watering his plants and doing this TV program, and then I got married again. This new guy was gay. He was gay at a time when, if somebody had known he was gay, they'd have shoved him in a hospital and given him shock treatments. It was 1960.

That marriage ended quickly, and I was faced with something that women from upper middle-class families were never faced with. I had to be a career lady. I had always thought I would stay home, my husband would earn the money, and I would do all the creative things. At that point, I was faced with, okay, now what do you do?

I applied to Stanford University, and I got a master's degree in journalism in 1964.

I had exquisite credentials. People who are reading this will probably think, ah, she wasn't qualified, but I was beautifully qualified! During the time that I was studying, I also did what's called developing a string, which meant that I wrote free features for every newspaper up and down the coast, every single one, including The Examiner and The Chronicle and the San Jose Mercury News, every single one of them.

I had a huge string, I was a proven journalist, and I was 32.

I couldn't get a job because they did not hire women who were 32. No paper would give me an opportunity to show that I could do the job, and I applied everywhere with Stanford University's employment agency behind me! I could not support myself. I had everything going for me, but a 32-year-old woman? No.

When I graduated from Stanford and I applied to all the newspapers in the area, I also applied to a public relations firm. I didn't want to, but I needed a job. I met this young man, and we went out for lunch, He said, "What do you have to drink?" and I said, "Oh, I don't drink." He replied, "Well, you'll never make it in this business." Every week, we would meet for lunch, and we would talk about job opportunities while I was selling dollar flaps. Do you know what those are, dollar flaps?

They were the golden books in Macy's toy department – and me with two master's degrees. We would talk about our job opportunities. This was in San Francisco. After a year and a half, I said to him, "You know, in a year and a half, there have been openings in your firm, why haven't you given me a shot at it?" He just blew me off.

Flash ahead from 1965 to 2019, and I am doing comedy in a place called Top Secret. I'm very funny, and the audiences in that particular club really like me. When I walk off the stage, they follow me off the stage, and they come out and hug me and kiss me and tell me that they want to be like me, which is crazy because they don't. I'm shot, and I'm funny looking, but they all say, "I want to be like you."

I asked the owner of the Top Secret comedy club, "Why won't you headline me when I do better than anybody else on your bill every single time for eight years? Eight years, I've been doing the lowest paid spot on the bill, eight years!" For the first two, I wasn't paid at all, but now I do the lowest. "Eight years, why won't you headline me?" He blushed, and he said, "Well, I pay you the same thing," which he doesn't. But he did not want to put my name on the website as a headliner.

That's how many years later? Times have not changed. That was the same exact thing I got with the public relations firm. Same thing. "We like you...but..."

We think that times have changed; women are screaming more, making more of a fuss, but we still hit the same wall. I am not where I want to be in standup comedy, and half the reason is that I'm a woman. We think that makes no difference. But look at Elizabeth Warren, that wonderfully capable woman who was knocked out of the race! We aren't ready to give women a level playing field.

Because I'm 86, and I do comedy on a comedy bill where I'm older than everybody else on the bill by about 50 years, I am a hit. Everyone says, "She is wonderful," but I am locked into the lower level of the comedy spectrum. And that's my story. I am finding a way to make myself seen and make myself visible, so that women who are younger than I will not have that problem when they try to be standup comedians. And I am seeing it.

Sixteen years ago, (I started when I was 70) there was a guy that used to do touring. I remember he would not give me a gig because he said, "I'm not going to have a 70-year-old woman driving the highways at night. You've got to have jokes, you've got to have jokes." And I see men that don't have jokes that get on because they're pushy, and because they have expensive PR and they have money.

I see these women that you see too, that are flashing their boobs around and talking about how hot they are in bed and how many blow jobs they give by the minute. They are getting ahead simply because they're shocking. They don't have jokes. People that do have jokes are furious because standup comedy is an art. You've got to have that timing, that almost innate sense of what's funny.

You listen to Carla Clay, who is not big, because she doesn't really want to make five times the effort of a man. She's a natural, so funny. Then there's Aundrea the Wonder woman, also so funny! They're not big because they haven't made that effort, since, as a woman, you have to try five times as hard. As a black woman, you have to try ten times as hard to get someone to look at you.

Age should never be a roadblock to your dreams. So you didn't take the leap in your 20s or 30s. You still have time! Pursue what you desire and don't let anyone tell you no.

–Sharon North Pohl

26. Julia: Seize the Dazzle

Stevia

"Make your lives a masterpiece, you only get one canvas."

-E.A. Bucchianer

When I had my daughter, I stopped writing. I tried for a year to stay in the loop with poetry and keep writing, and I had a writing group that I would bring her to. We would meet and discuss the poems, but as she got more mobile, it was too distracting, and for the first time in my life, I found writing and poetry really self-indulgent. It felt like I didn't have the bandwidth for it anymore. Poetry is the love of my life, so that was really shocking to me.

As she got a little bit older, I would do art projects with her. I always saw the world poetically, that never stopped, but the ability to have a quiet moment when there wasn't something else to do...it was rare to have any moments like that.

So what I did was I infused my daughter's life with art. She took this stamp pad, turned it over, and started printing on paper with it. She was using it "wrong." And it looks so beautiful. I took her papers, and I made these little series of rectangles. Then I started to make little drawings inside of these little rectangles, and I would put words with them. Pretty soon, I had 100 little rectangles...

You can try to stop the creativity, try to push it down, but if you are a creative being—you know this—it's going to find its way out. And you may not be able to predict what media will emerge. For me, it launched itself into visual arts. It kind of saved me. It let my brain not have to be so focused or quiet. It was something that fit into the kind of wildness of having children and navigating all of that. It really saved me.

Another thing that saved me was going on a writing retreat to the New Camaldoli Hermitage in Big Sur, California, twice a year. I just made the commitment that in this time, in the craziness of my day, I will find a way to make sure that the muse has not left my universe because I knew that was still important to my soul.

I think a lot of women get into the role of just giving, giving, giving, and then there's nothing... At some point, I had this image of an empty bowl, and it was like you can't... you just...there's nothing to scrape from it!

There's nothing to scrape from it if you're constantly giving.

Find one thing that's just for you. Something that you loved when you were a girl, or a moment in time where you felt more alive doing something, or when time disappeared and you let yourself do that thing, and let yourself not do it well. Let yourself do it ugly.

Give yourself a few moments of writing. Write with your non-dominant hand if you need to, so it doesn't have to be perfect - it's innately imperfect. But give yourself something.

Collage is an easy way to get creative without it having to be so perfect. Give yourself a minute of creativity. Make a quick collage, or sit down and write for 10 minutes, non-stop, stream of consciousness. Do that for a week, for two minutes. Creativity heals, baby.

Making art accidentally turned into a job. One of the moms said, "Why don't you...? There's an opening for art teachers here after school." For three years, I taught preschool art, which was like corralling a bunch of kittens with paintbrushes. That was an exciting time, me and ten preschoolers with paint.

For me, that experience was coming back to the essence of not overthinking, of finding that pure, distilled joy of creation and getting lost in it. That's what those kids taught me. It let me give new people on the planet a beautiful first experience with creativity.

I was a founding member of Poetry Santa Cruz. When I came back to Santa Cruz, one of my professors said, "I want to take you to lunch." I thought, "Oh shit, here's a professor who's hitting on me. What am I going to do? This is weird. It's awkward." I just immediately thought the worst.

At that lunch, he invited me to publish my first book of poetry. He said, "Whose book do we want on our shelves? Who among us may not have the publishing gene?" I was invited to put a collection of poetry together, and that was really exciting.

I've won the Mary Lambert Smith award and have been published in the Review almost every year for a long time. That's been a nice way to stay anchored a little bit in poetry and be part of it. I will never let Santa Cruz go. It's where my poetic past lives.

I didn't know how all-consuming it would be to be a mother, and having done it now for 13 years, I've asked myself, "Why did I do this? Why'd I think that I could be this?" And you know, there have been times when I have just failed miserably. There have been days where I've been cruel, unavailable, or selfish.

To reconcile that and be okay being a mother and being human, sometimes you just need to let the basic things be enough. Set the art materials out on the table, set the food out, provide the basic things, and don't judge yourself. It is challenging to be a creative person and a good mother because so much of art is just taking that time. Nothing gets made if you're not sitting and doing the making. Being forgiving in all of this, giving yourself grace, is a massive part of it...Don't lose your inner artist, but don't get turned into CPS for neglect.

Where do you hit the flow in your life? For me, it's horses and coaching. I don't paint, but I plant flowers. Is that art? I don't play an instrument, but I foster transformation... Is that art? My point is that art is that place where it seems the universe is writing something beautiful and just using you as a pen. So, relax... you've got plenty of ink.

-Sharon North Pohl

27. Gunilla: Cleverly Creative

Vanilla

One should always play fairly when one has the winning cards.

- Oscar Wilde

The backstory here is that I was embroiled in a bitter, long, hard, and miserable custody battle with my ex-husband. At this point, I was remarried, and my ex-husband was just fighting me every step of the way. We finally had 50/50 custody (which is a Good Thing[TM], and all I ever asked for) of our two daughters, an older and a younger that are a year and a half apart.

My older daughter was in middle school. She did not want to do one week on, one week off. She preferred to have some solid time with me, and then go to her dad's house and have some solid time there. My younger daughter, however, did not want to be away from her multiple pets at either home for more than a week.

For the longest time, we kept talking to my ex-husband, trying to get him to agree to something different, but if I even said as much as, "Hey, can we look at doing something with the schedule?" I would get shut down immediately. If the girls asked, he would assume that it came from me and, therefore, say no by default. It was incredibly frustrating!

At one point, he had to have oral surgery for an impacted wisdom tooth or some such. I happened to be talking to him on the phone and saw an opportunity. I said, "Hey, why don't we try this thing: I have both the girls for one week. Then the youngest goes back to you for a week, for which I keep the oldest. Then I get the youngest back, and the oldest goes to you for one week, and then the youngest goes back to you and you have them both for a week."

He said "Sure, that sounds kewl", and I was beside myself! I knew full well that the only reason he agreed was because he was doped up on pain meds after the oral surgery, and he was wasted out of his mind. People have asked if I ever felt guilty. The answer is no. On paper it looks terrible, but I know that the only reason he was resisting in the first place was because I was the one suggesting a change.

Our new arrangement was two weeks on, two weeks off for my oldest, and one week on, one week off for my youngest. This resulted in 50/50 time with the kids, but half of that time was with only one kid! I had one week with both, one week each kid, then one week no kids. I got that awesome one-on-one time with middle school girls, getting to focus on just the one kid at a time, while still having equal time with both of them.

I know this led to us having a much better relationship. They got individual time and attention, which, to kids that always were thought of as twins because they were so close in age and looked alike, was quite a treat. They both told me things I know they would not have shared with me if the other sister had been in the room, or just around the corner.

They were always close, and in fact, they still are, but it's undeniable that this arrangement meant less fighting. Spending some time apart did wonders. I am assuming that their dad had similar experiences with them at his house.

I guess the moral of my story is if you must get creative in your means of getting your ex-husband to agree to something that is clearly in your children's best interest, then so be it. I have no regrets.

We're not always going to be wrong, and we're not always going to be right, either. Other people's opinions don't matter. What's important is how you feel about the choices you make and what they mean to you.

-Sharon North Pohl

28. Olivia: The Muse

Saffron

"The whole world is waiting. The whole world needs you."

-Sally Field

It is important to meet life standing up. Every day, decisions have to be made. If you make those decisions from your standing, they will be your most powerful. Know yourself well enough, and you will have the courage to walk away from that which doesn't serve you. Maybe, more importantly, you will know what serves you before you say yes or no. You will get more grace and a wider worldview. From that place, all of us can be of far greater service.

I was quite conspicuously the first divorce in the history of both sides of my family. It sort of equaled a scarlet letter. Even my parents, who didn't seem happy, stayed married until my father died. That's the model that I grew up in—till death do us part. You just stay together no matter what. They didn't fight; it felt to me more like a business arrangement. It's not that they were cold to each other. There was just no romance, no affection... not a happy life. I wanted to leave home, and in my family culture, marriage is the way a good girl does it.

If I were escaping the expectations, I would have just moved in with him in "sin", but I didn't. I married him because that is who I was then. As it turned out, it was not a union based on the love I really had to give or receive.

I got pregnant early in the marriage. I realized that I had made a big mistake; a home in which you raise a child should be filled with love, communication, and harmony. I wanted to get out, and I was afraid. "Oh my God, look, I had a baby right away, and my child is going to grow up, and he is going to be ruined by it, and I'm going to be stuck in this marriage!" I thought I should make that decision before my son was old enough to know, and I immediately realized, "Holy crap, If I'm going to get out, I need to get out now." That was huge for me and the second biggest decision I had ever made in my young life.

I wasn't honoring myself because my "self" at that point was still so very tied to *whatever* my family said. Every part of me felt like that was the thing to do. It was only afterward that I said, "What the hell just happened? I don't trust myself!" It just wasn't the true me. It was the "good girl" battling with a deeper me I knew little about.

I saw myself as a good girl and I had no problems with that. I had always been well-liked in school. I enjoyed school, but I also had dreams of seeing the world. I felt like I wanted something bigger, and I didn't know what it was.

My sister had rebellion down pat, and she paid a huge price for breaking with my parents' rules. I saw this happen, and being outcast terrified me. I had no idea I was really the wild child! I just felt that something was calling me, and it was crying to get out. It has articulated itself over the years in different ways. The first way I unleashed her was simply by getting a divorce in the first place.

Not being married all these years, I have led a rich life of experimenting - spiritually, geographically, sexually, and much more. I have overcome expectations, both in myself and from others. I think that many people live under certain unreasonable expectations, whether it's family, traditions, or just superstition. Look at the rules that you might be putting on yourself. I have had the space to try things, both wild and good, that might even be shocking to a normal relationship.

I was told young that it was a sin to give my own body pleasure and also a sin to give pleasure to anyone else. That simply was never true. What is true for me? Service, joy, connection, and harmony. However I find it. That's what I seek and express. That's what's true for me.

I'm made of stardust, and I think you might be too. It's time for us all to get back to the garden! Whatever you need to step more into your true self, I think is worth it. Getting out can be a real struggle, especially when you think you are trapped.

The real thing that drives my sexuality is discovery and love for harmony, communion even. Sex is about self-expression and connection. It hurts when I see someone who doesn't allow in how truly beautiful they are.

I have helped people make their choices more powerfully and with more awareness. One of the ways, which is surprising to many, is with something called "flogging." Yes, it's a BDSM term, but it's much more a ritual. A portal of sorts. It unlocks the inner conversation of needs, desires, and resistance too. I create an experience of safety and the space for others to let go and try on a new mantle of joy and release.

No, I don't just beat people with a cat o' nine tails, it's a sacred ritual that can be fun and adventurous, and it's an important time to talk about sexuality. Someone could have the leather just lightly touch them, and it brings up something that they would like to be free of. It can also signal a new beginning. I've watched many people set down heavy loads and choose freedom and joy instead.

I have enjoyed living without anybody else's expectations making me less than I am and manipulating how I am supposed to behave. We want to define everybody we know; we want to put them in a box, have an understanding of who they are. Sure, there is a certain stability in that. However, deciding that I was not going to live by other peoples' labels freed me to be adventurous and willing to push my comfort zone a lot more. I believe that's because no one was there to say the words "You can't" for whatever reason, no one to ask, "Aren't you afraid?"

I once worked with a lot of rock stars. I had a reputation for helping talented people, a muse, you might say. I didn't start it, but a tradition began where rock stars would give me a tiny lock of their hair; it became a symbol of good luck for a number of them. I am good luck!

There is a Chinese proverb that goes, "To know the road ahead, ask those coming back." The road ahead involves daring. From what is still unfolding as a wonderful life, I am here to tell you that if you honor your spirit of adventure, you will know the harmony that a fully integrated person knows.

I love the movie line: "If everyone says I'm wrong, I must be right." Do you follow your intuition over popular vote? Good. I'd rather be wrong than a prisoner of what others think.

-Sharon North Pohl

29. Michelle: But I Love Him

Hyssop

"But love is blind and lovers cannot see."

-William Shakespeare

My name is Michelle Jewsbury, and I currently live in bright and sunny Los Angeles, California. I grew up in a wonderful household where my mom and dad were loving. My daddy was military, so we moved around a lot, but I always knew that family was very, very important to me. I didn't witness any extreme traumas, and I didn't experience anything to make me go in a different direction.

Fast forward my life a little bit until 2011; I'm 30 years old. I met this blue-eyed, blonde-haired man who had it all. He was intelligent, very successful in his field, and he wanted to pursue me. I had moved to Hollywood to take up an acting career, and, at first, I was very hesitant to get involved in a relationship. I kept telling him no, and he kept pursuing. He sent me flowers and wonderful text messages. He took me out to ball games and had me fall in love with the Los Angeles Dodgers, which was really awesome. I love baseball.

His perseverance paid off, and I decided, "Okay, fine, I'll jump into this relationship with you." We started our romantic relationship around January 2012. Four months later, my head ended up going through the drywall. When they hear my story, a lot of people don't understand why I stayed past that first incident, let alone what came after, but Paul was, to me, my knight in shining armor. That incident made me feel that, hey, possibly, he was under stress. Possibly, I could have triggered him. Possibly, it was an accident.

We didn't discuss it. I just remember after my head bounced off the wall, he left the room, and I turned around and looked at the wall. All I thought to myself was, well, I need to patch that. I didn't bring it up again, I didn't talk to him about it. I actually had his friend help me patch the wall.

The emotional abuse got a lot worse. It didn't start with him telling me that I was ugly, hideous, stupid, or an idiot; it started with gaslighting. He would make me think and believe the way that he did, and not the way that I personally remembered any situation.

He would come at me and say, "Well, you are a great actress, but that's not going to give you any type of reward in the end, and you're going to end up on the streets." It was a compliment, but it was a backhanded compliment, where he would tell me praise while also putting me down.

One huge catastrophic event that happened—roughly ten months after we started dating—was him, very intoxicated, thinking that I was flirting with another man. We were out at a Halloween party. He said he witnessed me talking to somebody else, came up to me, and grabbed my arm. I remember grudgingly following him down the gravel pathway to our car.

I knew he was too intoxicated to drive, but I also didn't want to upset him, trigger him, or make his attitude worse, so I got in on the passenger side. We swerved in and out of cars on the freeway, driving home. I remember it was a chilly night. I stayed stoic and nonresponsive, quiet the entire drive home.

We got to the house, and he came over to the passenger side and opened the door, grabbed me by my hair, and ripped me out of the car. He dragged me with him to the front door, opened the door, and threw me inside. I remember stumbling forward and then looking behind me, looking at Paul, and I could not see the beautiful blue eyes; all I could see was black.

At that point, I knew I was in trouble. He started berating me, kicking walls, spitting on me, screaming at me. Eventually, he started physically assaulting me. He hit me in the face; he threw me through walls. His favorite tactic was putting the fingers of his right hand in my mouth and strangling me with his left hand. He pressed so vigorously under my tongue that I would bleed. I don't know why that was what he went to most, but I think it was a control factor. I think that really gave him power, whether I lived or died, power over how long I could breathe.

I managed to break free from him a couple of times during that incident; one, in particular, I ended up running down the road. I remember hearing him behind me, his breathing, his heavy breathing. He was taller than me, and I was running as fast as I could. He still caught up with me, grabbed my hair, and threw me down. I sobbed, and he kept telling me to shut up and be quiet. I begged him, "Please don't hurt me anymore." He said, "I won't. I just want you to come back to the house so we can talk." He grabbed me by the back of my neck and led me to the house, threw me inside, and the onslaught continued.

At this point, I had been beaten for roughly four hours, and he started getting his consciousness back. He put me in the shower with him, rinsing the blood off of my body, out of my mouth. I was too weak to lift my arms to wash my hair. I was stoic, dazed, confused, and he laid me in bed and held my hand, maybe thinking holding my hand would stop me from running, but that was the last thing I could think about.

I drifted in and out of consciousness. The following day, when I actually woke up, he stared at me, and he began to sob. He was crying because my face looked like I had just completed a 10-round boxing match. He cried and begged me for forgiveness, told me that he would never do it again, and he was so sorry; he didn't know what had come over him. I believed him. I thought that it wouldn't happen again, but lo and behold, it did.

He started manipulating my mind. For example, if we got into an argument, he would tell me later that I remembered it differently, that it was my fault for triggering him or making him upset, and that I was hysterical and needed help. This ongoing manipulation lasted roughly four years.

I stayed with him because there's a cycle of domestic violence. That cycle goes from walking on eggshells to a big blow-up, whether that be physically, emotionally, sexually, and then the apology stage.

This apology stage is what typically keeps victims trapped in abusive relationships because a) the victim believes that the abuser will change, and b) the abuser at that point in their life, when they are saying these words, they really believe that they will too.

Everybody who leaves abusive relationships typically do because they have reached a breaking point. I got to mine when I discovered that he was having affairs on me. At that time, subconsciously, I allowed him to hurt me physically, violate me emotionally and sexually, and abuse me financially. But cheating on me? That I couldn't take.

I tried to break free. We talked through a lot of things, and he actually let me go... not for good, but so I could get my head back on my shoulders and re-evaluate our relationship. I think he hoped that I would come to my senses and come back to him.

I went to Los Angeles, and at that point, I started writing. I started documenting things that happened to me, still in constant communication with Paul. We spoke multiple times a day, text and voice. He wanted me to come back, but he had also jacked up over $50,000 in debt on my credit cards and leased a vehicle with my name that I couldn't afford. I was trying to figure out a way to get out of this debt that he had me in and not trigger him to where he would just walk away from me.

When I started writing, I began to understand how bad it was. When you're involved in an abusive relationship, you typically will address the now and how you're going to survive, you don't look at how it's all happened before and will happen again. You don't understand or realize how bad it is while you're in it.

After I had left and started writing, I knew that I needed to speak up. It came out in a play format; I wrote a 65-minute solo show. Before performing the play, I remember receiving a message via Facebook from a woman Paul was seeing at that time. (I was still in constant communication with him.) She reached out to me and said her head just went through the window in our bathroom.

At that point, I had to make a tough decision. I had already written the play, and I was rehearsing to be able to perform it. But like I said, I was still talking to Paul. I had to figure out, do I break ties with him completely, let my credit go to crap and speak up, or do I let him continue controlling my life?

This woman decided that she wanted to move forward and prosecute him for what he did to her. I chose to be a voice and stand up next to her. It took a lot of strength and courage on many levels to do that. I had been manipulated, but at that point I was writing, I did understand, I was rehearsing, and I was trying to figure out how to break free.

I let my worries about my credit and finances disappear, and I made up my mind to stand up against Paul. I decided to press charges. The statute of limitations was over in my case (typically two years in California), but I was able to press civil charges against him. The other gal pressed criminal charges.

I sent Paul an email in December of 2015, stating that I found out what he had done and that I was going to stand up against him, and I didn't talk to him again.

I ended up debuting my play scared. I was so terrified to do this. I hired two bodyguards to protect me and my audience during this play and debuted it in February of 2016, with a nearly sold-out audience. At that point, people started coming up to me and saying, "It's amazing how you've been able to speak up about this. Your story impacted me, giving me the courage to leave my abuser."

I started thinking to myself, "Wow, there are so many people around the world that have experienced this type of trauma. We really need to put a stop to it!"

I performed my play again later that year at the Hollywood Fringe Festival. Afterward, I ended up setting it down and going to Italy, where I decided I would turn my play into a book. I wrote my book, finishing it while I was in Italy, drinking wine and eating lots of pasta. It was titled, *But I Love Him*, the same as my play, and it was my personal experience in my abusive relationship.

Although I had finished my book during that trip, I was scared to publish it. I held on to it for another year, primarily because of some of the legal issues we were facing. In the meantime, however, I was called to start a nonprofit organization to help survivors worldwide. I remember traveling to San Francisco interviewing for a nonprofit, but it didn't feel like a fit. The next day, I walked around San Francisco, had clam chowder and a glass of Chardonnay on pier 39. A gentleman came up to me, and we started talking. I told him my story. He said, "You need to start a nonprofit." I remember thinking to myself, well, this is not the first time I've heard this, so this is the time I should listen.

In July of 2017, I decided to start "Unsilenced Voices." We were a 501(c3) within a month. I was in Ghana a couple of months later, and we now impact thousands and thousands of individuals in Ghana and Sierra Leone, Africa. We are a fiscal sponsor for an organization in Nepal, as well as working on providing programs and resources to survivors here in the United States of America. I knew at that point that my voice needed to continue to be heard.

I published my book in 2019, right after my case had settled, and I remember feeling exhilarated and on top of the world because I could speak up against an injustice that happened to me. When I published that book, I regained my voice. From there, people started coming up to me more and asking me to help. I decided to pursue a speaking career where I could coach and support individuals worldwide.

I speak specifically about overcoming obstacles because everybody faces obstacles, and everybody needs to overcome them, be they stress or anxiety, child abuse, domestic violence, or rape. We have all as humans experienced something, and that something needs to be spoken about in order for us to heal.

If we don't speak up, if we stifle our emotions, we cause ourselves physical and/or emotional ailments when we get older. It comes up as autoimmune disorders, chronic fatigue, headaches, chronic pain. If you don't talk about the things you've experienced in your life, you will have turmoil later in your life.

I teach people how to overcome that. I am so excited to be able to spread my message of hope, of recovery, of teaching people that you are enough, that you can turn your adversities into assets, that you can turn your lemons into lemonade because I did. I am no better than anybody else. Everybody can turn their lemons into lemonade, and they can turn their thorns into beautiful rose bushes. I love being able to teach people to do this.

When we feel stuck or lost, it's often because we're following a code that doesn't align with who we really are. Shed the rules from past relationships and your upbringing. Your zest will shine when you embrace your truth.

-Sharon North Pohl

Garlic

30. Beth: Daughter of Comedy

"If a man does not keep pace with his companions, perhaps it is because he hears a different drummer. Let him step to the music which he hears, however measured or far away."

-Henry David Thoreau

I am Beth Freewomon. My mom sang on Broadway. When she met my dad, and they got together, the improv club was kind of a child to both of them in a way. That is an interesting story in and of itself, and for another time.

Mom really was in show business. My dad wanted to be a producer in show business, so this coffee house for the theater people was born. That's how it started, a place for the people, my mom and her colleagues, to hang out.

A big part of the legacy of my family is show business. I guess what I would call courageous is that I really found my own way... not necessarily in the face of great adversity, but in the face of just not going with the default. Even my stepbrothers all got into some form of showbiz.

I went to art school in San Francisco, San Francisco Art Institute, and I had so many creative, wild friends. I ended up co-hosting for a short while—my foray into some form of entertainment—a cable TV show with my friend, whose character was Vegas Griff.

I guested as his co-host a number of times. I made up a character and a name, Luna Freewoman, which was kind of a mockery of who I actually was to become. That's part of why I kept that name, although I didn't change it legally. I did this cute little fun cable TV show for a little while, really just a handful of times.

After I finished college, I associated in the community with women who were very woman-identified and connected to a more divine feminine spirituality. I had been sexual with both men and women in college, but I ended up identifying as a lesbian, and very woman-identified.

That's where my name kind of stuck. That's why it's an O and not an A, Freewomon with an O at the end. I've been the black sheep of my family, and I've just stayed in my power and stayed empowered.

I feel like people have come around to understand a bit of what I'm about and embrace me spiritually, politically, and sexuality-wise. Even my dad finally came out as a father of a lesbian once it was starting to be trendy.

Releasing expectations is a great way of having a good day. The best way I know is to want what I have instead of having what I want.

-Sharon North Pohl

31. Noel: First on the Bus

"You better treat her like your queen, if you want to be treated like a king."

– Moosa Rahat

I wrote my book, "King Lessons," and brought 40 men together with one question in mind: "How do we honor women more fully?" Some of the men in your lives may enjoy the read. If the men in your life have served you and honored you, please acknowledge them. Just remember, so many of us want to suit up and show up for you if you allow us.

"Showing up" means getting my light turned inward and then turning back out. When we "Get out" we are engaging it like an engine. It radiates, and you draw good things to yourself.

I started first grade from the Sarah Fischer Orphanage. They had a yellow '40s school bus to take the kids to school. It was parked with the door open. I was a half-hour early getting on the bus, and I was the only child there. Moments later, a nun who worked in the kitchen boarded the empty bus and in her hands was a little treasure chest.

She handed it to me and said: "Every year on the first day of school, I give a treasure chest filled with goodies to the first child on the bus on the first day of school. This way, that special child will always remember that showing up early isn't early at all. I can tell you that, in this case, the rest were all late."

I learned that magic happens when I step up. My friend Sharon has stepped up, and her taking on writing this book shows that she has a treasure chest to give you! She has a treasure map of your life, and she will find that treasure in you. That's a big sister and friend. That's what I hope you are looking for in a coach because what I have found, in both myself and in Sharon's belief in me, is treasure.

To all the royal women reading this, I bow.

32. Ellie: Healing the Adoption Wound

Sunflower

"It has been said, 'time heals all wounds.' I do not agree. The wounds remain. In time, the mind, protecting its sanity, covers them with scar tissue and the pain lessens."

-Unknown

I always knew I was adopted. My parents read adoption books to me from the time I was little. I would picture my birth mother as a young woman with brown hair, parted down the middle, sitting in a field of yellow flowers, and looking sad because she missed me. These are my earliest memories of being adopted.

Adoptees often feel like their life began when they were adopted, and many of us have no sense of connection to being born. We hear no stories of our birth, have no pictures of ourselves from those first few moments of life, and no people around us that were present. Sitting in front of the mirror and staring at myself was a favorite pastime of mine. I had no genetic mirroring in my family, so I wondered whose eyes, eyebrows, hair, and facial structure I had. There was no discussion of where I came from, whom I resembled. I was floating alone in my world, disconnected from myself and all my ancestors. These deep questions haunted my childhood days.

The other part of my life that was a constant was my ability to dissociate and daydream. I spent many hours in my fantasy world. This was where I was comfortable. In this place, I was not in danger of being rejected again. In this space, I had no connection to the pain in my body from my relinquishment. I have come to find out that this is a common adoptee trait.

My search for my birth mother began when I was 22 years old. I discovered that she had written a letter to me when I was 17. That was the best news I had ever received. I was wanted! She would not reject me if I reached out!

The next two years of my life were consumed with calls to the adoption agency and pouring over the non-identifying information they sent me. I would read these papers over and over again, trying to match my handwriting to that in the forms. Was it hers? I did not know who filled out my medical information forms then, but I now know it was my maternal grandmother.

Unfortunately, the adoption agency could not locate my birth mother. She had been in regular contact with them, updating her address in case I was trying to find her, until the last two years.

The longing to find my roots took me down a rabbit hole, where I read every book I could get my hands on about adoption, search, and reunion. It was all I did on my downtime from work—no more hanging out with friends. I would lie on my bed, reading and crying every night until I fell asleep. All the adoption agency could tell me was that my birth mother's name was Sharon, and she lived in California. Legally, I was allowed no other information.

For two long agonizing years, I was stuck in a holding pattern, waiting for my birth mother to contact me. Coming home from work every day, I would run to the mailbox to check for a letter. When there was nothing, I would run up the stairs to my apartment and check the answering machine for a message. There was nothing. My heart would break a little bit more every time this happened.

The last time I called the adoption agency, I made a desperate plea for help. I told the social worker that I was at the end of my rope. I could not go on with this agonizing pain any longer. It was becoming difficult to function, and I needed to find my birth mother. She told me the only advice she could give me was to pray.

Taking her advice to heart, I came up with a strategy. Using a Japanese papier-mâché wish doll I received from a friend who had traveled to Japan years earlier was the cornerstone of my plan. I bought a special pen to draw in the dolls' eye. The story goes once the wish comes true, you draw in the second eye. The stage was set. On a warm August summer evening at sunset, I lit candles and listened to the haunting voices of African a cappella singers surrounding me as I held my doll. I prayed and cried with everything I had in my heart and soul that my birth mother would find me.

This is the part of the story where I let it all go—no more checking the mailbox, no more checking the answering machine, and no more reading books and crying myself to sleep every night. I let it all go. I decided to have faith that this would work. I began living my life again. Five days later, I came home after being out with friends, and there was a note on my answering machine, "Sharon from California called."

Reunion stories are commonplace in newspapers and talk shows. They present a tear-filled, happy moment where both people's lives suddenly make sense. Puzzle pieces click into place and create the whole picture. I truly expected my reunion to go along those lines. There was not a lot of information about the emotional complexity of a woman who felt forced to give up her child reconnecting with a child that felt abandoned.

Upon meeting my birth mother for the first time I was shocked to discover that I was completely numb to the entire experience. Watching her walk off the plane and into my life brought me no sense of joy or completion. I was empty. Numb. I had waited 24 years for this moment, and now I was going to blow it by not being connected to myself or her.

Meeting her was an experience that I have no words for. I finally saw someone I looked like. We shared the love of weightlifting, which was fairly unheard of in the early 90's. We loved being in nature and traveling, things my adopted family did not. I saw that our pinky fingers were identical, as were our belly buttons. She also brought many thoughtful and meaningful gifts, one for each birthday she had missed. I tried to soak it all in, but my numb state was a barrier. After those four days of reunion ended, we went our separate ways. She invited me to move in with her. I had wanted to leave my home state anyway, so I decided to say yes. Gathering up everything I owned, I moved across the country to live with my birth mother and her mother.

I was welcomed with open arms in her family and my birth father's family. Subsequently, I was able to form close family bonds with both of my grandmothers and my birth father's sister. These relationships were uncomplicated and deeply satisfying. I had found my people that I fit with. After my lifelong journey to feel a kindred spirit with family members, this was gratifying and made me feel I was with people who truly were my genetic mirror. My deep-seated issues of abandonment and pain had no connection to these relatives. I felt an easy closeness to them, but the deep relationship I wanted with my birth mother was more complex and continued to be just out of reach.

My conception was not the one from fairytales of love but one of nightmares. Even though it was a story of a non-consensual event by a man that was in the throes of heavy drug use and prone to violent episodes, my birth mother told me all the details she remembered. This was so important to me. Trying to shield someone from their truth is just another lie, and it is critical that adoptees be allowed to know their full story when they are adults. I commend her for being brave in her confessions of what happened, as it was a terrifying and disastrous event in her life.

She also recognized that my birth father did not remain that same person as the years passed. She took me to meet him in our early days of reunion and allowed me to develop my own relationship with him without judgment. This was a priceless gift she gave me. Meeting my birth father filled in many gaps for me about my looks and personality traits. We are similar in some ways, and, for an adoptee, that is everything!

There is a phrase some adoptees use to describe the time when they are uncovering the truth about how their adoption has impacted them. It is referred to as "Coming out of the fog". This is a painful awakening that their adoption was not a beautiful event where they were chosen to make a family complete like they had always been told. It was an awakening that I had been left alone in the world, and no matter how long and hard I cried, my mother was never returning. If I had words to describe this preverbal feeling of fear, loss, abandonment, and loneliness, it would be something along the lines of catastrophic destruction of my body and soul.

In our first few months of living together, every night before bed, I would lie on top of her and listen to her heartbeat, just the same way my babies did with me. I had not heard that sound in 24 years and the combination of yearning and pain that it manifested spilled out of me in gut-wrenching tears that threatened to pull the very life out of me. It was equally healing and devastating.

I was uncovering this pain as I was simultaneously immersing myself in my birth mother's world and trying to build a relationship with her. This was a monumental task that took me to the edges of my sanity. I had to go back to that little baby and relive my trauma. I wasn't sure I could survive it a second time.

Specialists on early trauma have stated that there is no greater trauma in a person's life than being abandoned by their mother. It is our greatest need to be nurtured by the one who birthed us. Neuroscience has now shown that newborns are aware of who their mother is and any replacement of that causes a disruption in the baby's neurological system. Stress takes over the baby's body, and an implicit primal wound is established. No amount of caregiving will erase this. There is much talk in the trauma world about relinquishment being classified as a PTSD.

Getting married and having three beautiful children kept me busy for 22 years. I have an amazingly supportive and loving husband. My children have also been equally supportive and loving. They are all well aware of my struggles and have offered kindness and understanding to me throughout this journey. I could not imagine my life without them in it. They have been my rock through all my ups and downs. Through parenting my babies, I was able to heal some of my own pain. Looking deeply into the eyes of the young children that are my genetic mirror and bonding with their souls remains one of the highlights of my life.

After I was done raising my children, I suddenly had more time on my hands. This was when I became more aware of what I was really feeling inside. It was time to confront the broken pieces that had yet to heal. So how to move forward after all of this? Years of therapy and self-help books only did so much. The anger I was feeling for being left was not budging. I could not heal it, and I could not release it. Being stuck in a pattern of resentment and grief, I despaired of ever feeling whole.

This seething anger prevented me from having the one thing I had always wanted, a close and loving relationship with my birth mother. How could I move on from feeling so rejected in the first hours of my life? That answer eluded me for the first 28 years of my reunion.

At that time, my mother was moving away. My abandonment wound was triggered, and I could not stop crying. I cried every day for months before confiding in my friend, a counselor, that I needed help. She introduced me to IFS (Internal Family Systems) therapy. She told me to imagine my young self that is hurting and hold and comfort her as my adult self. This seemingly simple exercise allowed me to become aware of the fact that I was re-abandoning myself in times of stress, leaving my young self to suffer alone. By comforting and holding her close to my heart, she was able to find a place of calm. This is a technique I still use often, and it is just as powerful as when I first discovered it.

They say it takes a village to raise a child. It also takes a village to heal a child, even if that child is already an adult. The next phase of my healing came when I discovered an adoptee community online.

Reading other people's truths, their stories of abandonment and grief that sounded so much like my own, was the most validating experience of my life. I was no longer alone with these feelings. I shared my struggles about my anger, and the support I have received has been amazing. I am profoundly grateful for these groups. They provided me a safe space to voice my story, and the support I have received and given has been a blessing. Community is truly healing.

Many stories made me think more about my reality. Numerous people in my new community were dealing with secondary rejection by their birth mother or death before they could even meet her. Looking at my situation, I was grateful I had a living birth mother who was open and willing to be in my life despite me pushing her away for almost three decades. She never gave up on me. Instead, she held steadfast to our tenuous relationship, hopeful that one day it would grow deeper.

I found resources to further connect me to other adoptees. I listened to podcasts by adoptees about adoptees, and I found much healing in their words. I read books about adoption, and one in particular, "The Girls Who Went Away" by Ann Fessler, was a game-changer. This book about what birth mothers went through in the decades before Roe v Wade opened my eyes to the anguish my birth mother endured by family and society during this time in history.

My anger was receding, and hope for a new way of relating to my birth mother began to take shape. I sent away for my original birth certificate, the only physical evidence I possess about my birth. I applied for my adoption file. The same woman I spoke to on the phone 28 years ago, trying desperately to find my birth mother, was the woman that I was speaking to that day. I was able to update her on what happened over the last 28 years, and she read my adoption file to me. This was certainly an example of things coming full circle.

My file was filled with the truth of my birth mother wanting to be in my life. She tried many times to connect to me and let me know she was there for me if I wanted her. Even though she had told me these facts when we met, hearing them from the adoption agency made them real. My mother wanted me; she didn't want to throw me away. I was finally free from the bonds of my fury, and I reached out to her to let her know I was ready to let go of my anger and work towards the relationship we both craved.

Living life without rage and grief as the center of it is a new and fantastic experience. Freedom to feel the joy that exists in human connection has filled my soul, and I live life fully present. This creates a feeling that every day is amazing, no matter what it brings. Being grounded in my body without deep anguish lifts my spirit and fills me with hope for my future and my relationship with my birth mother. My heart is open to her now in ways I could not have imagined before. I am grateful to her for her unwavering belief in me and for patiently waiting until I was able to welcome her into my heart. It is never too late to open our hearts, heal our pain and rejoice in the beauty and joy of being alive.

33. Sharon: Reunion

"I loved you for a long, long time. I know this love is real. It don't matter how it all went wrong, that don't change the way I feel. And I can't believe that time's gonna heal this wound I'm speaking of. There ain't no cure for love."

-Leonard Cohen

I would always look at young girls and wonder if they might be my daughter. I'd look in their faces, look at the shape of their hands, their eyes. I'd think, "Maybe this is my daughter?"

Throughout the years, I kept in touch with the adoption agency. I tried offering to help pay for my birth daughter's college education. I wanted to see if I could leave my assets to her. I got no response. When I knew that my birth daughter, my only child, the one I named Ellianna, was turning 18. I sent a letter for the agency to pass on to her adoptive parents to give her so she could find me if she wanted to. I sent medical information. I didn't ever hear back from them in all those efforts over the years. Later I found out that her adopted father threw the letter away. I never heard from her.

I moved from Sacramento, California, to Santa Cruz in 1989. That was the year of the Loma Prieta earthquake, which devastated Santa Cruz. I had closed escrow on my home in the Santa Cruz mountains a week before the earthquake. The house took massive damage, and I couldn't move in for the entire year it took to rebuild it. I got busy and distracted and didn't contact the adoption agency for a few years.

During that time, unbeknownst to me, my daughter had started looking for me. I had not updated my information with the adoption agency. She would call the Boys and Girls Aid Society, the company that had handled her adoption, over and over to see if I had any contact with them.

In 1992, I got myself organized, and I called to ask about my daughter. They told me that she had been looking for me. I gave them my contact information and waited. I was so excited. I had a lot of trepidation about what a reunion would be like.

At the time, I was taking care of my elderly mother, her grandmother. My daughter called one evening when I was out, and my mother answered the phone. My mom said, "We have been looking for you!" The first person my daughter talked to from her birth family was her maternal grandmother.

I got home too late that evening to return the phone call. I spent a sleepless night wondering what that first meeting would be like. I was excited. I was scared. I was on an absolute high about meeting her! What would she look like? What would she sound like? What color was her hair, her eyes? Was she tall, or was she short like my mother? Was she pretty? Did she go to college? She's now in her early twenties; what does she like to do? What is her work? Is she like me? The answers to those questions took another 25 years to reconcile and really get unwrapped.

We talked the next morning. It was the fall of 1992. She told me she was a physical therapist. She was living in Chicago, working at Cook County hospital in the trauma center. It was a tough county hospital catering to the underbelly of Chicago. I found it serendipitous that she was drawn to the same type of hospital where she was born.

We decided to meet at her childhood friend's home in Memphis, Tennessee. This would be a neutral place where her adopted parents wouldn't be close, so she felt safe to meet me. I will never forget getting off the plane. We were wearing similar black dresses and similar jewelry. The tilt of her head, the bone structure of her face, the shape of her legs, her pinkie finger; they were all mine. She was shorter and darker than me but unmistakably blood of my blood and bone of my bone. My emotions were overwhelming; my joy was overpowering.

I spent a week with her and her childhood friend. I brought her a birthday card and a small gift for each birthday that I had missed. I found out that she was unhappy in Chicago, making poor life choices in her friendships and relationships. She wanted out of that city and had always dreamed of moving to California. I offered her to come and stay with me in Santa Cruz. She took me up on it. In a matter of weeks, she had sold everything and came to live with me in Santa Cruz.

We took a trip to the big island of Hawaii shortly after she arrived. I arranged for her to meet her birth father, who was living there. I stayed in touch with his family over the years, remaining close friends with his sister and mother. I tried to stay reasonably in touch with him. I worked hard to find a spot of forgiveness for him. I wanted my daughter to be able to have the opportunity to meet her birth father as well.

We stayed in a small cabin at the foot of the Haleakala Crater on the big island of Hawaii. It was a magical place. We got to know each other on that incredible mountain. I had just had knee surgery, so I was on crutches. She was able to help me with some physical therapy. Ever since, I have referred to her as a medicine woman. Shortly after that, she changed her name from Cindy, the name that her adopted family gave her, to my name for her, Ellianna. She ceased contact with her adopted parents for years.

That first year was a challenge. Ellie had a mental breakdown. Her response to me was totally mixed, and she regressed to clinging to me, staying close to me, not wanting me to leave her. She was conflicted, with mixed emotions of extreme excitement and anger, deep-seated anger from the primal wound of me giving her up as an infant. I decided not to go back to work. She wasn't well, and she needed me in the way an infant needs their mother. I can't explain it; it was as if she became a small child again.

It was difficult financially, but we managed, and we managed together. We got creative and made it through that year. That winter, when we needed money, we became vendors at the San Francisco flower market. I had a big ranch that had a lot of holly on it. We cut holly, harvested pinecones and redwood branches, and made wreaths for Christmas. It was hard work. We had to be in San Francisco at 4:00 a.m., and it was an hour and a half drive, so we loaded up the night before. We would arrive with the branches in my horse trailer and unload in the wee hours of the morning. We did it together, and there was a sense of camaraderie and togetherness that I will never forget. She spent that year with me, healing and getting her mental clarity back.

The following year she met her husband, and shortly after that, they got married. He is a great guy, and he helped her get stable again. She's been here in the Santa Cruz mountains for 23 years now and has three beautiful children, whom I have helped birth and raise. My beautiful grandchildren are all young adults, and the joys of my life, born from my darkest tragedy.

I have been with her, dedicated to loving her ever since the day we met in Memphis. She has always kept an emotional distance from me, close yet far away. She couldn't let go of the abandonment issue of me putting her up for adoption. I was closer to her husband and her three children than I ever could get to her. I understood and stayed in that relationship, accepting whatever she could give. I never could break through. I just had to love her the way things were and recognize that her deep birth wound may never go away.

Just this year, however, a miracle happened. She ended up signing all the papers for the escrow on the long-awaited sale of my ranch with a power of attorney. This was the first time that she felt the world really knew that she was my daughter. She used to say, "There's no legal document linking us together." That experience, as well as her getting some adoption support from online groups, changed her perspective.

She has recognized how unusual and extraordinary our relationship is, compared to many other adoptees. There are stories of reunion and rejection by birth mothers who never told their stories, who hid the truth all these years. Some find they started searching too late, and their mothers are deceased.

Her kids are grown, and she finally has some time for herself. She has realized that I have been with her longer than we were apart, as she is almost 53 now. Finally, she has let go of the fear that I would leave her again. That pre-verbal baby never understood how her mother could leave her. That kept her at what she perceived as a safe distance from me for decades. She would sit across the room from me, her arms folded, staying out of reach.

One day a few months ago, it dawned on her that she is only hurting herself with this behavior. I am now in my 70s; how much longer will I be here? She has ultimately decided that I'm not going to leave her, and it is OK to return my unconditional love. She has finally forgiven me.

If there is a moral to this story, it is that some really bad things turn out to be blessings in disguise. From the mud blooms the lotus. Some things are worth waiting for, no matter how long it takes. None of us know how long we have on this planet. The black bamboo seed takes five years to germinate. When it finally breaks through the earth, it grows up to 5 feet in a single day.

I encourage all of you reading this to tell your story, to heal your story so that you can live a fully zesty life. Get Up, Get Dressed, and Get Out there today. The clock is ticking.

-Sharon North Pohl

34. Sharon: How Living My Get Up, Get Dressed, Get Out Philosophy Saved My Life

On my way back, on the returning flight from a speaking engagement in Cancun, Mexico, I started feeling a little bit sick. I'd come for my grandson's graduation. I never got to that ceremony. When I got to California I had a really bad cough and that cough went from being a little bit sick to landing me in the hospital with a rare form of pneumonia. The doctors couldn't identify what strain it was and what antibiotics would work against it.

That rushed me into intensive care and I went into a coma. I was on life support for two weeks while they were trying to figure out what was wrong and how to identify an antibiotic that would work. During that time I was intubated and on dialysis. It was a life-and-death situation. While I was laying there hooked up to so many tubes, fighting for my life, one of the nurses in the ICU suggested that my daughter make a poster for me of all the things that I had loved to do; all of my travels around the world and my activities. All of the events that I had participated in and loved.

She looked at him and said, "What good is that going to do? My mom's in a coma and she can't really see it."

At that point the nurse said, "It's not really for your mom, it's for us. All of us caregivers really would be more fans of your mom's if we understood what she was fully capable of and what she was like before she got in this position."

So my daughter made a beautiful fluorescent pink poster of me traveling and skiing, riding horses, playing tennis and doing all the things I love to do. Showing me fit and active. I was anything but that as the doctors and nurses were looking at me, trying to decide whether I was going to live or die. I ended up getting sepsis, which is total body organ failure so it was touch and go. I was given fentanyl. At the two week point I started to make a turn around. That poster moved with me to all the hospital rooms I was transferred into. It inspired my caregivers and made them fans, rooting for my full recovery.

That was the beginning of me starting to get better. When I came out of the coma I was shocked at how sick I'd been and how incredibly weak I had become. I wasn't really aware of my own condition and didn't even know what day or month it was! All the drugs, especially fentanyl, had taken a toll on my mental acuity. That took months to overcome. I

I ended up staying in the hospital for over two months. During that time I wasn't able to even get out of bed or lift myself up. When I finally got out of the hospital two months later, I could barely walk. I had to be lifted into a wheelchair and walked with a walker for the first few weeks. Finally I began to walk with an all terrain wheeled walker. Next I walked with a cane with 4 prongs. Then with a regular cane.

My doctors and caregivers (and there were many): cardiologists, kidney doctors, pulmonologist, rehabilitation, venous specialist, and therapists; occupational, speech, physical, mental acuity. They all told me that I may be on dialysis the rest of my life and that it would be unlikely for me to ever be able to play tennis, hike or to ride a horse ever again. I believed in a different narrative and I believed that wasn't the truth. I wasn't going to live my life on dialysis nor as an invalid.

I did everything I could to believe that this wasn't going to be the end of my life as I had known it. I did affirmations, I did all kinds of meditation and belief work. I knew how strong I'd been coming in, both physically and mentally, vital and full of zest. I believed that I could be that strong coming out of this medical emergency.

I worked diligently in rehab with all the therapists to regain my strength. Rehab is one of the hardest things I've ever done!

But today, four months later, my kidneys are functioning normally. I'm playing tennis, hiking, and traveling. I'm getting all my vitality back.

My daughter and my life partner were my best advocates and were with me daily through the whole trauma and pushed me to recover. Their belief and the reserve of fitness and mental resolve that I went into this health disaster with were key to getting back to my old life. I'd been healthy, fit and at a healthy good weight prior to this illness, with a positive mindset and a belief that I could accomplish just about anything. Those attributes are what saved my life. The belief and the physical strength and mental reserve that I went into this darkness with, were my arsenal I needed to fight my way back out. That reserve saved my life.

Since that experience I've been even more motivated to mentor other women and help them find their way out of their challenges. Things will come up in life because hard things will happen, hopefully you won't have a life-and-death experience like I did. You will have challenges though. I know from my experience that going into whatever tough things that are going to happen in your life with an ample vitality reserve is key. You will need both mental and physical vitality. Good self-care is the key to creating a strong body, a good healthy weight and a strong mindset. These aren't just nice things to have. These attributes are what could save your life! The Get Up, Get Dressed and Get Out lifestyle.

Here's a note I received from my granddaughter, Alleaha:

"I'd like to remind you how grateful I am that you are my tough, brave, badass grandma. I don't know what I would do without you, but thank God I don't have to think about that.

You've always been a fighter perhaps more now than ever and that's what might have saved your life. Most people in this condition wouldn't have gotten out; but you said hell no it's not my time to go yet. I'm so grateful for what you've taught me and so many of your qualities that you instilled in me have helped me be strong in my life."

I remember a sign I saw painted on a battered food truck in Sint Maarten, after the hurricanes, Irma and Maria had taken the islands in the Caribbean down to a huge rubble pile from an unknown St. Maarten Vendor. It said:

"You don't know how strong you are until being strong is the only choice you have."

-Sharon North Pohl

Story Salon

"When one definitely commits, providence moves too, arising in one's favor all manner of assistance and coincidence, which would not normally have come her way."

It's important to trust the process. I invite you to write your story by answering the next few questions. Please be specific! Recall the places, smells, sounds, colors, etc. Then, I want you to email it to me or call me and read it to me. Please make the commitment to share this with me. This is where the magic happens!

1) What is your earliest memory of knowing that you "can", that you have the will and the power to do anything? In other words, the first time you realized you had mojo?

2) Tell me a story about a time you crashed and burned, and please tell me how you recovered.

3) Recount a time that you were a hero, but pick a time you haven't told many people about.

4) What woman in history is your greatest influence?

5) What is a talent you have that you have kept secret?

6) What are your top 3 superpowers?

7) Go back and read your answers, and then write me a story designed to make me smile.

To share it with me, make an appt to call me at:

https://ZestyChange.as.me/ZestAsses

or email your story to: Sharon@ZestyChanges.com

EPILOGUE

"She won't stop. She's on a mission. This intent to do well keeps her demons at bay."

—Troy Garity about his mother, Jane Fonda

Get Your Free Guide

Scan the QR code to get free tips, recipes, and guides.

www.zestychange.com/guide

Discover Community

Scan the QR code to join my Facebook sisterhood, where you'll be surrounded and uplifted by inspiring women every day.

www.facebook.com/groups/zestywomen

Connect with Sharon

Scan the QR code to get your free 30-minute Zest Assessment, where Sharon will help you identify key ways for you to rejuvenate your zest in one aspect of your life.

https://ZestyChange.as.me/ZestAsses

z

Spices

Caveat: *I am not an herbalist. Botanicals are powerful. Please consult with your medical practitioner before starting any botanical regime. Any recipes, hacks and supplementation I discuss here are what I have chosen to use or do for myself, personally. Please do your own research and responsible consultations.*

Herbs and spices have been used for various medicinal purposes for thousands of years. What is listed here is a mix of historical beliefs and my own personal experiences, not strictly scientific facts. I use botanicals extensively to enhance my well-being. I found them invaluable when I was caring for rescued horses and their many ailments. Botanicals have also been my go-to help with the challenges of menopause caused by waning estrogen.

Below are the herbs and spices from the book illustrations, along with a few more:

Arrowroot, suitable for gluten-free diets, promotes weight loss, helps treat diarrhea, and strengthens your immune system.

Bay, use as a warming rub for sprains, anti-rheumatic.

Basil, boosts the immune system, use for colds, anti-diarrhea, kidney health.

Borage, use for fever, cough, and depression.

Cayenne (Capsicum), use for rheumatoid arthritis (RA), osteoarthritis, and other painful conditions.

Cilantro (Chinese Parsley), diuretic, sedative.

Cinnamon, lowers blood sugar. It is antiseptic, anti-diarrhea, helpful for diabetes or irritable bowel syndrome.

Cloves, topical anesthetic, toothache anti-dyspeptic (indigestion).

Chervil, diuretic, expectorant, tonic gives a sense of well-being.

Coriander, antispasmodic, diuretic, anti-inflammatory.

Cumin, anti-microbial, for colds, anti-emetic, motion sickness, nausea.

Dill, anti-flatulent, anti-colic, galactagogue (promotes great mothers' milk).

Garlic, better blood pressure, lowers cholesterol, reduces risk of heart disease, helps colds and flu.

Ginger, astringent, reduces insomnia, increases immune system, favored by royalty.

Hyssop, tea helps relieve respiratory infections, the common cold, and sore throats.

Lavender, helps with insomnia. The antioxidant activity of lavender may also contribute to wound healing.

Lovage, digestive aid, relieves flatulence and other stomach discomforts, in addition to helping digestion.

Lemon Zest, antimicrobial and antifungal. May boost your immune system and promote heart health.

Lemon Grass, reduces fever, is a pain reliever, stimulates the uterus and menstrual flow, has antioxidant properties.

Marjoram, indigestion, colic, anti-inflammatory, antimicrobial properties. Used to treat digestive issues, infections, and painful menstruation.

Mint, expectorant, for colds, local anesthesia, anti-spasm.

Oregano, go to spice to try for many ailments, antitussive (cough relief), anti-rheumatic, vermifuge diuretic, deodorizer.

Parsley, contains many powerful antioxidants, which may help prevent cell damage and lower your risk of certain diseases.

Pepper, considered the king of all spices, expectorant, anti-microbial.

Peppermint, believed to have a calming effect, helping with depression-related anxiety.

Rosemary, antioxidants, and anti-inflammatory compounds, thought to help boost the immune system and improve blood circulation.

Saffron, most commonly used for depression, anxiety, Alzheimer's disease, dysmenorrhea (menstrual cramps), and premenstrual syndrome (PMS).

Savory, antispasmodic, sedative, anti-parasitic, diuretic.

Sage, antiseptic, gastroenteritis, sedative function, memory.

Stevia, a natural non-caloric sweetener.

Sunflower, seeds are a superfood, rich in healthy fats, protein, anti-oxidants, anti-inflammatory, vitamins B1, B6 and E, supports the immune system and heart health

Tarragon, diuretic, anti-parasitic, emmenagogue (increase menses flow)

Thyme, expectorant, sore throat, colic, arthritis, upset stomach.

Turmeric, anti-arthritic, anti-oxidant, reduces inflammation.

Vanilla, calming effect, curbs sugar intake, rich in antioxidants.

Sharon's Five Hacks for a Zesty Life

"The Secret of Your Future is Hidden in Your Daily Routine" —Mike Murdock

GET UP:

Tips to start the day:

1. Do the 5 senses meditation for 5 minutes: sight, sound, taste, touch, and smell. Notice each of those things first thing in the morning, before you get up.
2. Keep a Gratitude journal. Write down 5 things you are grateful for. Read your list daily.
3. Write down/read five of your amazing accomplishments.
4. List/read who inspires you.
5. Acknowledge, write, or read 5 ways you have given back.

GET DRESSED:

This is about self-care, your mind, body, spirit, and your surroundings:

1. Juice a half lemon and rub on your hands and face to reduce age spots. After the lemon, rub 5% Greek yogurt (it must be full fat, not reduced fat) on your face. Why? It tones and brightens the skin, protects from UV-rays, increases elasticity, reduces fine lines and wrinkles, and fights acne. Leave on for 15 mins, and rinse with cold water.
2. Do some stretching, followed by 5 minutes of exercise to get your metabolism revved up for the day.
3. Drink the half lemon's juice with warm water, a teaspoon of apple cider vinegar, organic honey or molasses, cayenne, and turmeric. Beware: it tastes terrible! Why drink it then? Because this concoction boosts your immunity, turmeric is an anti-inflammatory (inflammation is the cause of a lot of joint deterioration and discomfort), and cayenne boosts your fat burning.
4. Take your vitamins.
5. Beautify: do one thing to make your surroundings more appealing. Your house, your garden, your closet? Choose an outfit that speaks to your zest. Wear things that make you feel

zesty, like the radiant queen you are. Choose something besides black!

GET OUT:

This one is about physically getting outside and moving, as well as getting out of your comfort zone, stretching your life experiences, and contributing.

1. Go outside every day for 5 minutes or longer. Just take a walk.
2. Get outside your comfort zone. Take a class, do one thing you have never done before.
3. Get out in the world and connect with others, friends, and family. Call one person a day.
4. Interact in a positive way with a stranger you cross paths with, in the world, or on the phone. Make their day better for having talked to you.
5. Find ways to give back. Reach out, volunteer, donate, recycle, stop using single-use plastic, bring your own bags when you shop, use less, eat less meat, join a movement. The earth needs all of us to stand up for her. She is on fire, and we are the firemen and women who can save her.

As we push past 50, many of my clients, as well as every other woman in the world, can use a little help against the effects of waning estrogen. I have put together a complete guide called "The Treasure Map to the Fountain of Zest". If you email me, Sharon@ZestyChanges.com, I will send you a free copy!

I include some recipes and herbal tips and tricks from my book. These are to help reduce anxiety and hot flashes, control weight gain, and let you feel sexy again.

Specific herbs contain ISOFLAVONES, also known as phytoestrogen, which mimic the actions of estrogen to communicate with your hypothalamus, and answer metabolic calls from your bodily functions, previously the job of estrogen.

When these natural herbal extracts communicate with your hypothalamus and the rest of your body, it makes your hypothalamus think your estrogen is balanced. Diet and herbs can make a huge difference in how menopause affects you.

Feel less anxious:

These herbs and supplements have a calming effect. As our bodies change, we feel less comfortable in our own skin. As a result, we lose confidence and feel more anxious. Here are some things that may help:

Take a food-based supplement:

For ease, take a complete all in one that has omegas included. The rice bran-based ones are best. (I use Zeal!)

Try herbal remedies:

- Green Tea
- Guarana
- Yerba Mate
- L-Lysine
- Ornithine (an Amino Acid)
- Phosphorus
- Ionic & Fulvic minerals.

Hot Flash Support:

As we go through menopause and produce less estrogen, our hypothalamus gets out of whack. It can no longer communicate with the ovaries. This lack of communication causes our symptoms: hot flashes, anxiety, brain fog, low energy, and dwindling libido. Phytoestrogens available in plants and herbs can help restore that communication.

- Ashwagandha and Bacopa
- A phytoestrogen powerhouse diet with lots of greens
- All soy-based products: tofu, soy milk, tempeh
- Veggies: broccoli, Brussels sprouts, cauliflower, yams
- Enjoy a glass of red wine or grape juice every night
- Legumes and seeds, especially sesame, flax, soybeans

Weight gain in menopause:

As our metabolism slows, we need to focus on revving it up. The way thermogenic plants and spices help is by boosting natural metabolism, reducing food cravings, managing calorie absorption, and impacting fat storage. Add these to your smoothies and everything you cook!

- Black Pepper
- Cardamom
- Cayenne
- Cinnamon
- Cumin
- Garlic
- Ginger
- Green tea
- Turmeric

Feel sexy again:

Some herbal supplements may help with your libido, your sexy self. After all, this is your time to enjoy yourself! You can't get pregnant, no more cramps, no mom and dad guilt. I favor Icariin (horny goat weed)

Herbal supplements:

- Maca Powder
- Icariin (Horny Goat Weed)
- Red Ginseng
- Dong Quai Root
- Maca Root
- Ashwagandha Root
- Sarsaparilla Root
- Epimedium

Some of my go-to recipes:

Keto coffee, frothy like a latte:

Brew your favorite coffee. If you use creamer, add it. For sweetener, try stevia or a little of the half stevia, half honey that is available now. Finally, add about a half teaspoon of organic unflavored coconut oil.

Blend it with a stick blender/mixer in a deep cup in the sink (cleverly avoiding a greasy coffee mess on your counter), then pour into your coffee cup. Voilà! Enjoy your frothy coffee; no need to drive to Starbucks.

Benefits of coconut oil: it increases heart health,

increases good cholesterol, is anti-bacterial, reduces appetite, and the ketones in coconut oil may boost brain function.

Simple, quick smoothie:

- Zeal vitamin powder (over 50 botanicals and vitamins in a whole food rice bran base)
- Protein powder
- Milk, milk substitute, or water
- Organic mixed frozen berries

Complex smoothie (My breakfast most mornings!):

- Zeal Vitamin powder
- Protein powder
- Milk or milk substitute
- Greek yogurt
- 1/2 banana
- Scraping from inside of peel (great for ulcers)
- Fresh ginger, a couple of slices
- Fresh or frozen kale
- Fresh Turmeric root (about ½ inch)
- Frozen mixed organic berries
- Ground chia seeds
- Ground flax seeds
- Ground whole oat groats
- Matcha green tea
- Moringa
- Baobab powder

- Maca root (mixed colors)
- Fresh Turmeric root

Go-to Cabbage Soup, suitable for Lunch or Dinner

If you eat chicken, save the bones in the freezer, and when you are ready, make some bone broth stock. Cook for an hour or more. Reserve some diced chicken. If you are vegetarian or vegan, use vegetable stock. If you want beans for your protein, make sure to soak them first.

In a separate stockpot, sauté 1/2 yellow onion and ten garlic cloves in olive oil until brown. Add diced turmeric root, diced ginger, black pepper, cumin, coriander, and Mrs. Dash as a salt substitute, the prepared strained broth, and any hard veggies sliced into bite-size pieces. Use what you like: carrots, turnips, parsnips, jicama, yams, etc. If vegan, use vegetable broth add soaked beans or other protein now. Cook on medium/low heat for about 20 mins, add celery and half a head of sliced cabbage, cook another 20 mins.
If you want to add soft, quick-cooking squash, asparagus, etc., do that now, along with your reserved diced chicken or meat substitute protein. Cook an additional 10-15 mins.

I cool and freeze in glass containers of about 2-3 servings. It is always available as a nutritious, low-calorie meal packed with protein, herbs, and phytoestrogens.

Kale Salad

I make a huge bowl of this, always ready to keep me from those chips. It will last for days in the fridge if you don't put your soft veggies in when you make it. Just hold off on the cucumbers, tomatoes, and avocados until you are ready to eat it, which is also when you should add your dressing.

Strip fresh kale, not baby kale, off the rib and chop it up. Massage it with virgin olive oil, or else it is really tough. Add carrots, celery, onions, pumpkin seeds or sunflower seeds, and raisins. Enjoy with your favorite dressing, Greek yogurt, or lemon juice.

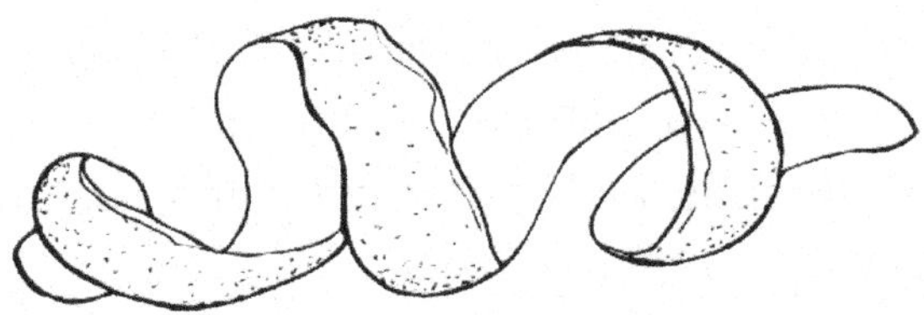

Acknowledgements

Mom

To my mother **Ellen Pohl** who always believed in me and instilled in me the life practices and system that showing up was key. She had zest, and showed me that I had inherent zest and could do anything I was willing to work for. Through example she thrived, despite an alcoholic husband who never fully supported his family. My mom at a young age gave me the foundation to realize the world needed our commitment to the planet. Thanks to her, my awareness of the precursor to climate change started over 60 years ago. We gave to the Save the Redwoods and the World Wildlife Fund before climate change was a topic.

Dad

Herbert Pohl was an alcoholic, a gambler, a womanizer, and my dad. He taught me how to forgive the unforgivable, love the unlovable, and keep getting up, no matter what. It took me years to quit choosing men just like him. I worked for him in his sporting goods business. He taught me entrepreneurship and business skills. He made me tough. He taught me how to survive adversity and thrive in distasteful situations.

Sister

To my sister **Valerie Gray**, my rock, the one who has always been there for me through all the times; both the zesty ones and those that weren't so zesty. A big sister, a surrogate mom, a midwife, a friend, a traveling companion, a financial supporter. This woman has never missed a beat in standing by me through thick and thin. I would not be who I am today (the good parts) without her in my court.

My Other Sister

Peggy Alexander, the sister of Ellie's father (whom I never married). She has been an undying friend since 1967. Peggy was there through all the drama and social revolution of the '60s. She has kept me and my daughter's family connected to her large Italian family. She helps me remember how tumultuous those times were and how crazy and scary her brother was. She validates my memories of unbridled youth and helps me make sense out of scattered memories.

My Ex Husband

Tom taught me to forgive the unforgivable, over and over again for 21 years. He taught me to take the high road even when he did not. He taught me that a man with an unsavory mother will struggle with treating women fairly their whole life. He taught me money is no substitute for love. He taught me that, despite his diminished capacity, he did the best he could to love me. Tom was generous, until he wasn't, loving until he wasn't, thoughtful until he wasn't. Our divorce dragged on for almost 9 years. He was a master of moving the cheese. He helped me break my pattern of choosing emotionally unavailable men with a mean, selfish streak. My lesson in perseverance: never give up, and go high when others go low!

My Zest Mate

Lawson Kilgallen, my zesty man, my reason for living, who has believed in me and supported me throughout the birthing of my company, Zesty Changes, and this book. The first truly healthy man I have ever chosen. I call him ultra-normal. It's the best re-run ever. We were a hot thing in our youth in the mid-'80s. We met climbing in Yosemite Valley. We reconnected on the eve of Tom's walking out of our marriage. A bonus: he taught me how to play tennis and gave me a 9-year adventure of living in the Caribbean Islands. Now he has been instrumental in the completion of our dream: to retire to the Gulf Coast of Florida. BTW he had a great mom!

My Daughter

Ellianna Ray Javed is my birth daughter. I met Ellie when she was 26. I gave her away at birth, my story is in here and you know the drama of that.

Ellie's been living near me or with me ever since we met. I've been with her through the birth of her 3 children; they were all home births.

Her family, her husband AJ and the 3 kids Isaac, Alleaha, and Luke have been instrumental in supporting both of us through our journey through these years. Ellie has been there with me and finally has been able to really connect with me. It took a lot of hard work, tears and struggle but we are there now.

She was so powerful and so supportive when I got sick this last year and was in intensive care. Ellianna was my biggest cheerleader and she was there every day. I want to honor where we've been and where we are today as a mother and daughter. We have finally arrived as true loving supporters, friends, and mother and daughter.

-Sharon North Pohl

Make Connections

Some of our zesty storytellers:

Angel Tuccy, Media Specialist
https://vedetteglobal.teachable.com

Chineme Noke. Transformational business coach, founder of Unstoppable Shepreneurs
https://www.linkedin.com/in/chinemenoke/

Dee Collins, self-publishing expert, CEO Predestined Publishing
https://predestinedpublishing.com

Gini Trask, Travel Expert
https://toptiertravel.com

Janet Calieri, https://janetcaliri.com/

Lauren Cohen, International lawyer, investment advisor, author.
https://ecouncilglobal.com

Merri-Jo Hillaker, Life Coach
https://merrijohillaker.com

Michelle Jewsbury, Philanthropist and founder of nonprofit Focusing on Stopping Abuse Against Women
https://unsilencedvoices.org

Susie Clark, author, Director at Kit and Kaboodle, an event and production company in England.
https://www.kitandcaboodle.co.uk

Tracey Ferrin, author, life coach
https://traceyferrin.com

Tracy Boone, grief specialist, founder Elijah's Path to Healing Foundation
https://elijahspathtohealingfoundation.com

Sharon: Don't Drown in Your Story

The telling of, and healing from, your story is a life-or-death matter. Just about a week ago, I had a soul shattering experience.

I answered a phone call from Washoe County, Nevada. I don't usually answer those calls, but this time I picked up for some unknown reason.

A man's voice asked, "Are you Sharon Pohl?" I thought, ok, here goes, somebody wants to sell me something or redo my website... I hesitantly said, "Yes." He said, "Do you know a Douglas Baker?" I paused, a flash from the past. I answered, "Well, my first ex-husband was Douglas Baker." He continued, "Do you know his middle name?" I replied, "Yes, his name is Lee." The man asked, "Was your ex about 66 years old?" and I said, "Yes." He went on, "Well, I'm sorry to tell you that Doug died in the county hospital yesterday, and we are looking for his next of kin."

I fell on the floor and asked if he could tell me a little bit more. He gave me some details. He was calling from the county coroner's office and needed to find someone to sign Doug's death certificate. I doubted that I would be that person; I hadn't seen Doug in 30 odd years.

I found out that Doug had been in-and-out of the hospital the last few years. Living in a homeless camp in Reno, Nevada, it seemed he got in a big fight and broke his hip. He was in the hospital for about a month and then suddenly died. They didn't know exactly why he died, but his health had not been good.

I can't tell you what a gut-punch that was for me. Here was a man whom I loved dearly. He was a gorgeous specimen; 6' 6", blonde-haired, blue-eyed, handsome, funny, intelligent, fit, creative, intelligent, a guitar player, and a singer—an Adonis!

He had a story, though, and that story rotted him from the inside out. It turned him into a drug addict, a drunk, and a gambling addict. It was the reason I ended up divorcing him. I spent $30,000 to put him through a treatment program and paid him alimony to help keep him clean and sober and on the right path. Still, I just could not make a dent in whatever it was that was eating at his soul.

Hearing where he ended up is a testament to how important these stories are and how critical it is to get them out in the daylight! We need to heal them, to look at them, to share them. Finding and defining a path so that you are not living your story is a life-and-death situation.

-Sharon North Pohl

So, What's Your Story?

Here are some blank, lined pages for you to start jotting down your own story! We want to hear it too, so if you want to share it with us, and maybe see it in the next book, submit it to the website: www.ZestyChanges.com

Or email.me

Sharon@ZestyChange.com

And don't forget to get your free guide:
www.zestychange.com/guide

I look forward to hearing your story!

You

Made in the USA
Las Vegas, NV
16 March 2023